■SCHOLASTIC

Comprehension Strategies for English Language Learners

Margaret Bouchard

New York • Toronto • London • Auckland • Sydney
Mexico City • New Delhi • Hong Kong • Buenos Aires

Teaching *Resources*

This book is dedicated to my parents,
Fred and Elvira Max, who taught me
early in life to value learning. This is
my wish for every child in the world.

Scholastic Inc. grants teachers permission to photocopy the reproducible pages
of this book for classroom use only. No other part of this publication may be
reproduced in whole or in part, or stored in a retrieval system, or transmitted in
any form or by any means, electronic, mechanical, photocopying, recording, or
otherwise, without written permission of the publisher. For information regarding
permission, write to Scholastic Inc., 557 Broadway, New York, NY 10012.

Cover design by Maria Lilja

Cover photo © Royalty-free/Corbis

Interior design by Ellen Matlach for Boultinghouse & Boultinghouse, Inc.

Interior photographs: page 4, Sequel Creatives;
page 8, Richard Hutchings; page 9, Maria Lilja.

ISBN 0-439-55428-4

Copyright © 2005 by Margaret Bouchard

All rights reserved. Published by Scholastic Inc.

Printed in the U.S.A.

1 2 3 4 5 6 7 8 9 10   40   13 12 11 10 09 08 07 06 05

Contents

Introduction

It is estimated that approximately 4 million immigrant children attend America's schools. More than 90 percent of recent immigrants come from non-English-speaking countries. This group represents the fastest growing segment of our student population. According to the 2000 U.S. Census report, one in five school-aged children in the United States is a nonnative English speaker—i.e., an English language learner (ELL). These statistics have a significant effect upon teaching practices and methodologies used in our nation's classrooms.

The challenges of helping English language learners (ELLs) succeed academically are profound. These students need to develop academic English language skills along with content knowledge. Very often nonnative speakers are placed in mainstream content classrooms with little help or support given to the students or the teacher.

Comprehension Strategies for English Language Learners is a collection of strategies that have proved to be successful for both mainstream students and ELLs alike. They are well suited for use in both mainstream content classrooms and English Language Development (ELD) or English as a Second Language (ESL) programs. These strategies are linked to the Goals and Standards outlined by Teachers of English to Speakers of Other Languages (TESOL), and are also research-based. (See pages 6 and 7 for a TESOL Goals and Standards correlation chart.)

Since every teacher is ultimately a teacher of language—whether it is the language of biology, history, math, or art—the content classroom provides numerous opportunities for teachers to expand the language skills of all learners, including ELLs. Many older ELLs do not have the luxury of mastering the English language before they must learn content material. Because it often takes years for these students to develop cognitive academic language skills (Cummins, 1981), it is important that content and language be taught simultaneously.

According to researchers, reading strategies considered effective for native speakers can also be beneficial for students reading in a new language (Fitzgerald & Noblit, 2000). However, ELLs may be so focused upon decoding the language that the use of strategies often plays a lesser role. This makes it necessary for you to teach these strategies explicitly and model them frequently.

Researchers also propose the grouping of learning strategies into three categories: metacognitive, cognitive, and socio-affective (Chamot & O'Malley, 1994).

Metacognitive Strategies Simply stated, *metacognition* means "knowing what we know," or to intentionally monitor our own thinking (Baker & Brown, 1984). It is characterized by a) choosing thinking and problem-solving strategies to fit specific learning situations, b) clarifying purposes for learning,

c) monitoring personal comprehension through self-questioning, and d) taking corrective action when comprehension fails (Dermody & Speaker, 1995 as quoted in Echevarria, Vogt, & Short, 2000).

Cognitive Strategies   Making inferences, visualizing, and predicting are all examples of cognitive strategies. With these strategies, a learner manipulates the material to be learned mentally (visualizing, for example) or physically (such as note-taking or creating graphic organizers).

Socio-affective Strategies   Cooperative learning and asking questions for clarification are examples of socio-affective strategies. These are strategies in which a learner interacts with one or more people in order to support learning.

You will find the strategy lessons in this resource are grouped according to the above criteria. In addition, the strategies found on pages 22–30 are those that work particularly well in the initial stages of English language literacy development.

Navigating the Lessons

In each strategy lesson, you will find

- the levels for which the strategy is appropriate,
- relevant research that supports the strategy,
- a definition of the purpose for which the strategy was designed,
- how the strategy benefits ELLs,
- step-by-step guidance through the lesson,
- key vocabulary, illustrations, and graphic organizers or other activity sheets, as necessary, to support learning concepts,
- sample progress indicators (right) to help you with assessment,
- ways to extend learning

Sample Progress Indicators for CODING TEXT

Student will:	A	IP	Notes
Use a coding system to mark text.			
Use the code to aid in comprehension.			
Develop a personal coding system.			

Each strategy lesson includes sample progress indicators to help you with assessment. You will find a blank progress form that you can customize on page 128.

This resource is designed to help you teach effective comprehension strategies to ELLs so that they may move beyond simply decoding words to improving their comprehension—and feel like an integral part of the classroom community. It is my distinct hope that it serves as a supportive and useful guide for all content teachers of English language learners and a benefit to the students they teach.

Margaret Bouchard

Correlation to the TESOL Goals and Standards

The TESOL Goals and Standards (1997) support the idea of teaching these reading strategies to English language learners. The strategies in this resource are aligned with the following goals and standards developed by TESOL:

GOAL 1 *To use English to communicate in social settings*

Standards for Goal 1

Students will . . .
1 use English to participate in social interaction.
2 interact in, through, and with spoken and written English for personal expression and enjoyment.
3 use learning strategies to extend their communicative competence.

GOAL 2 *To use English to achieve academically in all content areas*

Standards for Goal 2

Students will . . .
1 use English to interact in the classroom.
2 use English to obtain, process, construct, and provide subject matter information in spoken and written form.
3 use appropriate learning strategies to construct and apply academic knowledge.

GOAL 3 *To use English in socially and culturally appropriate ways*

Standards for Goal 3

Students will . . .
1 use the appropriate language variety, register, and genre according to audience, purpose, and setting.
2 use nonverbal communication appropriate to audience, purpose, and setting.
3 use appropriate learning strategies to extend their sociolinguistic and sociocultural competence.

For more information about the TESOL Goals and Standards, visit the TESOL Web site at http://www.tesol.org.

COMPREHENSION STRATEGY	GOAL 1 STANDARD			GOAL 2 STANDARD			GOAL 3 STANDARD		
	1	2	3	1	2	3	1	2	3
Using Illustrations to Interact With Text				■	■	■			
Frame Sentences				■	■	■			■
Summary With Illustrations					■	■			■
About-Point	■			■	■	■			
Think Alouds					■	■			
QAR: Question-Answer Relationships					■	■			
GIST: Generating Interaction Between Schemata and Text				■	■	■	■		
Reading Guide-O-Rama				■	■	■			
Question Guides				■	■	■			
Previewing Text				■	■	■			
Coding Text						■			
Herringbone Technique				■	■	■			
Opinion-Proof			■		■	■	■		■
Semantic Feature Analysis				■	■	■			
Guided Imagery				■	■	■		■	■
Anticipation-Reaction Guide				■	■	■			■
Mapping			■	■	■	■			■
Selective Highlighting and Note-Taking	■				■	■			
Using Graphic Organizers and Signal Words					■	■			
Question–Research–Outline–Write!	■			■	■				
Reciprocal Teaching				■	■	■	■		■
ReQuest Procedure				■	■	■			
Cued Retell—Oral or Written				■	■	■			
Peer Tutoring	■			■	■	■	■		■
Think–Pair–Share				■	■	■			■
Jigsaw Classrooms			■	■	■	■			■
Collaborative Reading and Alternative Texts				■	■	■			■
Content Rewrites and Adapting Written Text				■	■	■			
Leveled-Highlighted Textbooks				■	■	■			
Group Reading Inventory (GRI)					■	■			

Why Should Teachers Teach Comprehension Strategies in the Content Areas?

Comprehending and recalling expository material (like that found in textbooks) is a challenge for many students—both native and nonnative English speakers. The technical vocabulary of specific content areas, the numerous concepts presented, and the unique structures and features of expository text are new and challenging for many students. The challenge is even greater for English language learners. In addition to the language barrier and the need to understand expository text, they may face gaps in their background knowledge and be adjusting to cultural differences and a new environment. Clearly, the careful, explicit teaching of comprehension strategies for understanding expository text will benefit all students, including ELLs.

Research supports teaching these comprehension strategies during content lessons rather than in isolation. Charmot & O'Malley (1994) cite four reasons:

1) Content provides students with an opportunity to develop important knowledge in different subject areas.

2) Students are able to practice the language functions and skills needed to understand, discuss, read about, and write about the concept developed.

3) Many students are more highly motivated to learn when they are learning content rather than isolated language skills.

4) Content provides meaningful context for teaching learning strategies.

How to Teach Strategies

It is key to teach a few strategies at a time, and teach them well. The following approach for teaching strategies to ELLs is based on the research of Fielding & Pearson (1994) and Chamot & O'Malley (1994). The approach is also supported by Lev Vygotsky's (1962) theory of learning. Vygotsky suggests that students learn best when their learning is scaffolded. In other words, what a learner can do today with support, he or she will be able to accomplish independently in the future.

Teacher Modeling

1. Choose a specific academic task and a strategy that will help students achieve it.
2. While you work through the task, "think aloud," explicitly modeling the mental processes you use in applying the strategy.
3. Refer to the strategy by name and use that name consistently.
4. Explain to students how the strategy will help them understand the content and how, when, and for what kinds of tasks they can use the strategy.

Guided Practice

1. After you have explicitly modeled the strategy, give students more responsibility for task completion.
2. Practice the strategy with students.
3. Support students' attempts by giving regular feedback.
4. Have students share their thinking processes with other students in whole group, small group, or pair discussions.

Independent Practice

1. Encourage students to apply the strategy on their own.
2. Provide students with regular feedback from both you and class peers.

Evaluation

1. Have students self-evaluate the outcome of using the strategy.
2. Prompt students to ask, "Did this work for me?" and "What strategies work for me?" (They can write this in a learning log.)

Application of the Strategy

1. Give students the opportunity to apply the strategy to a new genre, assignment, task, or real-life situation.
2. Offer praise when students successfully apply the strategy to a more difficult task.

At times, students may find a particular strategy too complex or difficult for them. Often these challenges can be resolved by providing more instruction, examples, and practice. If this is not successful, you may want to develop a more simplified version of the strategy or choose another that is not quite as complex.

Things to Consider When Selecting and Teaching Strategies for ELLs

Cultural Background

Culture affects the way a person perceives, interacts, and thinks about the world. It affects every part of a person's being, including learning. The cultural traits students bring to the learning situation may affect their reaction to, or success with, a specific learning strategy. Therefore, it is helpful for you to be aware of any cultural influences that may affect student performance when implementing a specific strategy. The following are a few examples of cultural considerations that may influence student participation.

Cultural Adaptation: Cultural adaptation is the extent to which an immigrant has accepted and can successfully participate in a new culture (see the chart on pages 12–13). This process generally moves through sequential phases characterized by euphoria, followed by types of discontent followed by acceptance.

A student's level of cultural adaptation can affect his or her motivation, stress level, and success when executing a learning strategy. Consequently, it is important for you to continually monitor a student's level of cultural adaptation.

Gender: In some societies, males and females do not participate in certain types of mixed group activities. This may be due to cultural or religious ideas. For students with this type of background, participating in cooperative learning groups may be difficult.

Respect: For some cultures, it is deemed disrespectful to question a teacher. It is essential that both the student and teacher never "lose face." This may have an effect upon strategies that require the questioning of an instructor or where the student plays the role of the teacher, such as in Reciprocal Teaching.

Participation: In collectivist societies, students may only speak up in class when called upon personally by the teacher. These students may not readily share in a general invitation made to the whole class.

In order to understand the cultural characteristics a student brings to the learning situation, you might consult "Culture Grams," a product that contains information regarding numerous cultures around the world, or consult an ELD or ESL professional. (www.culturegrams.com)

Confrontation: In some cultures, formal harmony in the learning situation must be maintained. Therefore, expressing an opinion that might be contrary to those of the teacher or others in the class would not be an acceptable behavior. This may be a challenge for strategies that include sharing opinions.

Language: Students whose first language is a Romance language (for example, Spanish, Portuguese, French, Italian, Romanian) may have challenges with "chunking" or shortening language. This may effect their progress with strategies that require this skill, such as mapping, note-taking, and nonfiction writing.

English Language Level

Varying stages of English language development are characterized by specific skills (see the chart on pages 12–13. Therefore, a student's English language development level is directly related to the linguistic tasks he or she is capable of performing. It is important to choose and adapt learning strategies to complement the student's English language level and thus promote successful participation. For example, a student whose English language level is considered Early Production may need the support of a native language peer when participating in a strategy that requires a lot of verbal output.

Learning Styles

Each student has his or her own preferred learning style. ELLs are no different. The way in which we approach a task or a learning situation depends upon our learning style. Learning styles are a general predisposition, voluntary or not, toward processing information in a particular way (Skehan, 1991). Some students learn best by hearing information. Other students learn visually, and still others learn best through concrete experiences.

It is helpful when teaching content and selecting strategies to know the learning styles of your students. For instance, a visual learner may prefer and be more successful using graphic organizers than an auditory learner. An auditory learner may prefer a retell strategy, and a concrete learner may prefer handling objects.

I've provided two ways to help you assess a student's learning style. You can observe your student and then answer the questions on the Observational Learning Styles Inventory on page 17. If a student has sufficient English, you may want him or her to complete the Learning Styles Inventory on page 18. If the student cannot read, read it to him or her. If possible, ask a speaker of the

Stages of Language Development and

Stage I — Preproduction

Linguistic Considerations	Cultural Considerations	Suggestions for Teachers	Questioning Techniques	Effective Activities
Student . . . • communicates with gestures, actions, and verbal formulas. • builds receptive vocabulary. • recycles learned-language practice. • benefits from listening comprehension activities (e.g., audio recordings).	• silent period (i.e., a period of time when a non-English-speaking newcomer to the United States may only listen and not attempt to speak English—lasting from one month up to a year or longer)	• Create a stress-free environment. • Provide support and encouragement. • Avoid asking direct questions.	Appropriate questions and prompts include • Find the ___ • Point to ___ • Put the ___ next to the ___. • Do you have the ___? • Who did ___? • What is his/her name? • What is this (concrete object)? • Who is he/she? • Who has the ___?	• face-to-face conversation • following simple demonstrated directions • participation in art/music/physical education • use of manipulatives (i.e., puzzles, games, and real objects) • use of picture books • drawing

Stage II — Early Production

Linguistic Considerations	Cultural Considerations	Suggestions for Teachers	Questioning Techniques	Effective Activities
Student . . . • intuitively understands that English is a system. • labels and categorizes. • encounters first language interference (i.e., linguistic factors of the native language interfere with learning a new language —as with verb or modifier placement). • uses one- and two-word responses and chunks of language. • can say "I don't understand."	• adaptation fatigue (i.e., stress from efforts to adapt to a new culture leads to decreased motivation and increased frustration)	• Monitor error correction (i.e., use modeling). • Use anticipation guides. • Reiterate list of key terms for previewing. • Provide audio recordings of readings and lectures. • Organize information graphically.	Appropriate questions . . . • require a yes/no answer. • ask either/or.	• low-level questions • retelling a story • using picture books with simple texts • simple written responses • copying words and sentences • following recipes • oral reading • written practice

Cultural Adaptation

Stage III — Speech Emergence

Linguistic Considerations	Cultural Considerations	Suggestions for Teachers	Questioning Techniques	Effective Activities
Student . . . • uses language purposefully (e.g., to clarify or refute). • produces complete sentences.	• signs of culture shock may appear (e.g., manifesting itself in feelings of anger, distrust, loneliness, isolation, depression, or physical illness) • recovering from previous frustration and fatigue	• Use frequent comprehension checks. • Design lessons focusing on concepts. • Introduce expanded vocabulary. • Use models, charts, maps, and time lines.	Appropriate questions and prompts include • why or how (open-ended) questions. • specific questions • How is it that ____? • Tell me about ____.	• demonstrations • simple oral presentations • answering higher-level questions • hands-on activities • small group work • word sound symbol production • simple writing • computer lessons • play and role-playing • choral reading

Stage IV — Intermediate Fluency

Linguistic Considerations	Cultural Considerations	Suggestions for Teachers	Questioning Techniques	Effective Activities
Student . . . • produces connected narrative. • uses reading or writing incorporated into lesson. • writes answers to higher-level questions • resolves conflicts verbally	• cultural acceptance (e.g., manifesting itself in positive self-confidence while participating in new culture)	• Validate students' languages and cultures.	Appropriate questions and prompts include • What would you recommend or suggest? • How do you think the story will end? • What is the story about? • What is your opinion on this? • Describe/compare/contrast. • How are these the same or different? • What would happen if ____? • Which do you prefer? Why?	• content/subject explanations • paragraph writing • reading for information in content areas • summaries, outlines, book reports • explanation of new ideas/concepts • workbooks/work-sheets, tests • lecture discussions • literary analysis of plot, character, and setting • simple report writing

Adapted from Enst-Slavit, G., Moore, M., & Maloney, C. (2002). Changing lives: Teaching English and literature to ESL students. *Journal of Adolescent and Adult Literacy*, 46:2, 116–127.

student's first language to assist you in reading and explaining the inventory. When compiled, the answers on these inventories can point to a preferred learning style.

In addition to using these inventories, an interview or discussion with the student can provide information about how he or she undertakes a learning task. For instance, ask the student to respond in a learning log about how he or she would go about teaching another student how to solve a specific problem. Responses in a variety of situations can tell a lot about a student's learning style.

Planning a Content Lesson for ELLs

Student Inventory

Before starting a content unit of study, it is very helpful to gather information on the levels at which students are functioning. These levels include English language level, reading level in English, preferred learning style, and prior knowledge of the content.

Ask the ELD or ESL specialist in your district to provide you with an English language level for each student as necessary. This should include oral and written language, and a reading level. Also, find out what kinds of materials are available for students functioning at this level. If your school does not have an ELD specialist, ask the reading specialist to assist you.

The Student Inventory form (page 19) can help you plan for instruction and materials for nonnative speakers in your class. The following is a list of criteria included on the inventory and an explanation of why each is important:

First Language: The closer a student's first language is to English in structure and origin, the easier it will be for the student to learn English. For example, it is usually easier for a Spanish or Italian student to recognize English words than it is for a Vietnamese or Russian student.

Literacy Level in Native Language: If students are literate in their first language, they will have some prior knowledge about how the literacy process works. This knowledge transfers to second language learning. And if you or an assistant can read in a student's native language, knowing this literacy level can also help you choose for the student compatible materials that are written in his or her native language.

English Language Level: It is important to be aware of the English language level at which students are functioning. This level defines the linguistic skills students possess and the tasks they are capable of executing. Knowing students' English level will help you adapt strategies to coordinate with ELLs' ability to function in English. In addition, always choose lesson plan components keeping ELLs' English level in mind. This is particularly important for choosing vocabulary and lesson objectives.

Preferred Learning Style: As discussed earlier, each student has his or her own preferred learning style. ELLs are no different. Discovering a student's preferred learning style can help you choose the best strategies and activities to help the student succeed.

Prior Knowledge: Students bring their prior knowledge to the learning situation. Students from diverse cultures may bring very different experiences to the learning situation and struggle with text that has been written for the mainstream American culture.

Also, some students may have extensive knowledge of the concepts involved in a specific area but not the language skills in English to express this expertise. If possible, ask a person who speaks a student's native language to assess prior knowledge of a topic. If this is not possible, becoming acquainted with the curriculum a student may have covered is helpful.

Lesson Planning

When planning a content lesson for ELLs, the form on page 20 and the following guidelines may help you develop a lesson plan.

It is important to consider how you will integrate ELLs into the whole-class learning experience. Taking a little extra time to evaluate your expectation and results for these students will support accountability and lead to more successful participation.

Content Objectives: It may not be possible to cover all of your district's or state's content objectives, so choose the most important ones. It is often helpful to discuss your choices with a colleague. Also include process objectives for each content area.

Keep in mind the task-oriented knowledge that students need to know in order to meet the content objectives. For example, do they know how to construct a time line or read a map?

Vocabulary: Vocabulary choices should include technical terms specific to the content being studied. Also, look for opportunities to build background knowledge and to teach non-technical words that cross subject areas (e.g., words like *sequence* or *analogies*) to further enrich your students' vocabularies.

Language Objectives: Listening, speaking, reading, and writing constitute the categories of language objectives. Try to include each category in the lesson plan. For example, a listening objective could be as basic as "Listen to a tape of the Gettysburg Address." Or "Listen to another student read the Gettysburg Address." Speaking might be: "Give an oral report or retell to

another student the information you received from reading the time line."
Reading might include finding and reading a trade book about a topic or
reading a section of text. Writing might include keeping a learning log or
writing a letter to an expert source requesting information.

Learning Strategies: Include strategies from the three categories:
metacognitive, cognitive, and socio-affective.

Materials: Find opportunities to include authentic realia in the content
lesson. For example, if the lesson is about sea creatures, bring in actual
seashells for students to experience firsthand. Also, trade books and other
supplemental materials are helpful.

Evaluation: Use a variety of evaluation/performance assessments and include
student self-evaluation. Portfolios, learning logs, authentic assessment, and
the sample progress indicators are excellent methods by which to evaluate
ELLs.

Follow-up Activities: Review is essential. Use follow-up activities to reinforce
concepts that have been introduced.

Observational Learning Styles Inventory

Student: _____ Date: _____

Directions: If a student does not yet have the English language skills that are needed to complete the Learning Styles Inventory (page 16), this observational checklist can help indicate his or her preferred modality.

1. _____ Asks others to verbally repeat. **AUDITORY**

2. _____ Uses a lot of gestures. **TACTILE-KINESTHETIC**

3. _____ Refers to illustrations frequently. **VISUAL**

4. _____ Draws pictures. **TACTILE-KINESTHETIC**

5. _____ Repeats to him/herself. **AUDITORY**

6. _____ Uses bilingual dictionary. **VISUAL**

7. _____ Likes building, making things. **TACTILE-KINESTHETIC**

8. _____ Likes to listen to tapes. **AUDITORY**

9. _____ Writes/copies information on paper. **VISUAL**

Additional Observations: Ask a bilingual helper to assist you and discuss with the student how he or she learned best and studied in his or her native country.

Score			
	yes	no	sometimes
Visual			
Auditory			
Tactile-Kinesthetic			

Comprehension Strategies for English Language Learners   Scholastic Teaching Resources

Learning Styles Inventory

Name: _____ Date: _____

Directions: Answer the following questions. These questions will help tell how you like to learn. There are no right or wrong answers.

1. I like to draw or trace things. **TACTILE-KINESTHETIC**
   ☐ yes ☐ no ☐ sometimes

2. I learn best when I listen to other people speak. **AUDITORY**
   ☐ yes ☐ no ☐ sometimes

3. I remember best the things I read. **VISUAL**
   ☐ yes ☐ no ☐ sometimes

4. I really enjoy science experiments. **TACTILE-KINESTHETIC**
   ☐ yes ☐ no ☐ sometimes

5. I learn best when I say it to myself. **AUDITORY**
   ☐ yes ☐ no ☐ sometimes

6. I understand better when I see videos/filmstrips. **VISUAL**
   ☐ yes ☐ no ☐ sometimes

7. I like to make or build things about what I am learning. **TACTILE-KINESTHETIC**
   ☐ yes ☐ no ☐ sometimes

8. I remember best the things I hear. **AUDITORY**
   ☐ yes ☐ no ☐ sometimes

9. I like to use charts and graphs. **VISUAL**
   ☐ yes ☐ no ☐ sometimes

Score			
	yes	no	sometimes
Visual			
Auditory			
Tactile-Kinesthetic			

Comprehension Strategies for English Language Learners   Scholastic Teaching Resources

Student Inventory

Class: _____ Date: _____

Instructor: _____

Student name: _____

English
language level: _____ First language: _____

Reading level
in English: _____ Literacy level in
first language: _____

Preferred learning style: _____

Content unit: _____

_____

_____

_____

Student's prior knowledge about concepts in this unit: _____

_____

_____

_____

_____

Additional information: _____

_____

_____

_____

_____

_____

Lesson Plan
Integrated Content Instruction for English Language Learners

Content topic: _____

Content objectives:

Key vocabulary:

Language objectives:

Listening/Speaking:

Reading/Writing:

Comprehension strategies:

Metacognitive:

Cognitive:

Socio-affective:

Materials:

Evaluation:

Follow-up activities:

Comprehension Strategies for English Language Learners   Scholastic Teaching Resources

Comprehension Strategies

Using Illustrations to Interact With Text

ENGLISH LANGUAGE LEVEL

Early Production

KEY VOCABULARY

☐ caption
☐ chapter
☐ draw
☐ picture
☐ know
☐ page number
☐ question
☐ see
☐ title

RESEARCH BASE

Mayer, R.E., Steinhoff, K., Bower, G., & Mars, R. (1995).

Purpose   This strategy enables students to summarize the steps in a lesson, experience, or event. It provides the opportunity for them to access prior knowledge, ask questions regarding instructions or visuals contained in text, and interact with information from the content textbook.

Key Benefits for ELLs   This strategy allows you to assign meaningful content area work to beginning ELLs. In addition, they will feel a sense of accomplishment by participating in this cognitive activity. It is important from the outset that even beginning language students have the sense that they are active members of the class. This helps build self-esteem and confidence.

Procedure

1. Give students a copy of the Illustration Activity Sheet (page 23).
2. Show them where to write the chapter number and chapter name on the sheet.
3. Show students where to write the page of the illustration or visual.
4. Ask them to carefully study the picture.
5. Ask students to draw a picture of the illustration (picture or graph).
6. Show students how to copy the caption under the picture.
7. Ask them to write what they see in the picture. They may label any items in the picture they can identify. (This can be done in English by using a bilingual dictionary.)
8. Ask students to write what they already know about the subject. This can be done in English or their native language. (If possible, it is helpful to have students work with a bilingual partner who speaks the same language.)

> It is helpful for ELLs to use a bilingual dictionary.

9. Ask students to write or draw any questions that they have.

Sample Progress Indicators for
USING ILLUSTRATIONS WITH TEXT

Student will:	A	IP	Notes
Ask questions.			
Interpret visual information.			
Draw visual information.			
Access prior knowledge.			

Using Illustrations to Interact With Text

Chapter title: _____

Chapter number: _____ **Picture page:** _____

Draw the picture (visual or graph).

Caption:

_____

What I see:

_____

_____

What I know:

_____

_____

Questions:

_____

_____

Comprehension Strategies for English Language Learners Scholastic Teaching Resources

Frame Sentences

ENGLISH LANGUAGE LEVEL

Early Production to Speech Emergence

KEY VOCABULARY

Will depend upon the topic for the frame sentences.

RESEARCH BASE

McCracken, R., & McCracken, M. (1995)

Purpose   Frame sentences can be used to help students understand and build content vocabulary and develop awareness of sentence structure. They may also help you determine students' prior knowledge about a specific topic.

Key Benefits for ELLs   Very often it is difficult for beginning ELLs to express what they already know about a topic, in either oral or written form. Also, quite frequently they are unfamiliar with specific text structures, such as cause/effect, comparison/contrast, problem/solution, and question/answer sequence. Using frame sentences can help ELLs understand text and sentence structure while learning content information.

Procedure

Here's an example of how to construct sentence frames for the topic Plants.

1. To determine prior knowledge, ask: *What do you know about plants?*

2. Then introduce the frame sentence:

   Plants are living things that _____grow_____.

   Plants are living things that _____need water_____.

3. The sentence frame is repeated until students have finished writing their information.

4. After each lesson covering the topic, students can write in new information that they learned using the sentence frame.

You can construct sentence frames that enable students to use nouns, adjectives, verbs, and prepositional phrases.

Example:

Nouns: Elephants eat _____leaves_____.
             Elephants eat _____grass_____.

Verbs: Elephants _____spray_____.
             Elephants _____run_____.

Adjectives: Elephants are _____big_____.
             Elephants are _____loud_____.

Prepositional Phrases: Elephants live _____in the jungle_____.
                         Elephants live _____in herds_____.

You can also use sentence frames to highlight certain forms of text structure. If a unit of study involves a specific form, use sentence frames to aid students in understanding these structures. For example:

Compare/Contrast: If _____ , then _____ .

Cause/Effect: Because _____ . Therefore, _____ .

Problem/Solution: A reason for _____ was _____ .

Question/Answer: Who? _____ When? _____
Why? _____ Where? _____

Sequence: First _____ . Next _____ .
Finally, _____ .

For additional signal words and text structures, see the list on page 83.

■ ■ ■ ■ ■ ■ ■ ■ ■ Extensions ■ ■ ■ ■ ■ ■ ■ ■ ■

- Ask students to use the information from the sentence frames and make a Fact Sheet (page 26) about a given topic, which students can use as a study guide.

- Have students keep the sentence frames in a journal or notebook. This can be used as both a study guide and as an evaluation tool.

- Use student-created frame sentences to construct an informational paragraph. Delete specific content words from the paragraph and ask students to supply the correct word. You can use this as an evaluation tool.

Sample Progress Indicators for
FRAME SENTENCES

Student will:	A	IP	Notes
Use English to complete sentences that provide a variety of content information.			
Compare and classify information using technical vocabulary.			
Use prior knowledge to enhance content learning.			
Use the appropriate English grammar structures to convey meaning.			

Fact Sheet

Name: Date:

Directions: Use information from your frame sentences and write a fact for each one.

1. _____

_____

2. _____

_____

3. _____

_____

4. _____

_____

5. _____

_____

6. _____

_____

7. _____

_____

8. _____

_____

Comprehension Strategies for English Language Learners   Scholastic Teaching Resources

Strategies for Beginning Language Learners

Summary With Illustrations

Purpose   This strategy enables students to summarize the steps in a lesson, experience, or event by linking visuals with text. It provides the opportunity for students to put information in sequential order and express themselves via two modalities: the visual and the written word.

Key Benefits for ELLs   By using this strategy beginning ELLs can participate in classroom activities from the very beginning. The versatile nature of the activity lends itself to many venues, including the summarization of sections or chapters of text, events, a field trip, a math story problem, a science experiment, a narrative story, or any other topic you deem appropriate. For the beginner, the summary can be adapted easily to be as short as one sentence. It provides an opportunity for beginning language learners to demonstrate knowledge about a specific topic.

Procedure

1. Make an ample number of copies of the summary/illustration activity sheet. (Two formats for the activity sheet are included; one consists of two summary boxes, the other has four.)

2. Show students how to label the sheet, depending upon the nature of the assignment.

3. Demonstrate how to draw a picture in the box. For example, if a unit is about Antarctica and you are studying penguins, point to the picture of a penguin, then point to the empty box and pretend to draw the picture.

4. Next to the picture, show students how to write a simple sentence in English. For example, *Penguins are birds*. You can also allow them to describe the picture in their native language.

5. As an alternative, you may want to assign specific illustrations from a text for which a summary can be written. Or supply pictures of a process, event, or experiment. Students can put them in order, paste them in the boxes, and write a simple summary sentence or vocabulary to match. To use for description, they can draw a picture of a person, animal, or object and write a description next to the illustration.

■ ■ ■ ■ ■ Extension ■ ■ ■ ■ ■

When sheets are complete ask students to orally describe what they have drawn and written.

ENGLISH LANGUAGE LEVEL

Preproduction to Early Production

KEY VOCABULARY
- ☐ draw
- ☐ sentence
- ☐ summary
- ☐ write

RESEARCH BASE

Mayer, R.E., Steinhoff, K., Bower, G., & Mars, R. (1995)

Sample Progress Indicators for
SUMMARY WITH ILLUSTRATIONS

Student will:	A	IP	Notes
Draw a picture that coordinates with a written summary.			
Synthesize information.			
Write a summary.			
Place events in correct sequence.			

Summary With Illustrations

Topic: _____

Comprehension Strategies for English Language Learners Scholastic Teaching Resources

Summary With Illustrations

Topic: _____

Comprehension Strategies for English Language Learners   Scholastic Teaching Resources

Additional Suggestions for Teaching Beginning ELLs in a Content Classroom

- **Always give students a classroom textbook.** This communicates a sense of belonging and use of the text can be adapted to students' individual language level (see page 166).
- **Ask students to carry a "bilingual notebook"** to class. This can aid in vocabulary development. They can write key words in English and also in their native language, along with a definition.
- **Students can trace maps** or other visuals and label them accordingly.
- **Electronically record sections of text.** This can be done by asking native English speakers to read the sections. This can help with pronunciation and reading. Students can listen to text as a homework assignment.
- **Concentrate on the visuals** in the text: charts, graphs, illustrations, diagrams, time lines. Make a copy and omit some information. Ask students to use the text to "fill in the blanks."
- **Develop a collection of pictures** that coordinates with the textbook illustrations. Give students a picture and ask them to find an example in the text. For example, if you give a student a picture of a mountain, he or she then finds an example in the text and can write the word and the page on which it is found. Or you can give the student a group of different pictures and ask him or her to find an example of a key vocabulary word. If the word is ship, the student sorts through the pictures to find an example of a ship. You can provide a list of key words. After the student has found examples, he or she can show you or a learning partner.
- **Keep a supply of magazines.** Ask students to look through them and find pictures of key vocabulary. Then they cut out the pictures, paste them in a notebook, and write the words (and definitions, if possible) to make a content dictionary.
- **Look for content area books written in students' first language.** These can be a "bridge" to learning. Consult your ELD or ESL professional or librarian for help in accomplishing this.
- If possible, **ask a person who speaks a student's first language to make an audio recording in that language of key concepts** that you provide and would like the particular student to learn in his or her first language.

About-Point

Purpose This strategy is a tool to enhance comprehension for silent reading. It teaches students to identify what the content information is "about" and the "point" of the subject matter. Students stop at logical points while reading text and respond to the statement: *This section is about ____, and the point is ____.*

Key Benefits for ELLs About-Point is a useful strategy for ELLs because it uses small, manageable amounts of text and teaches students to identify both the content matter and the point of the information, while at the same time stimulating recall. Managing large amounts of information can often be a daunting task for ELLs. In addition, recognizing what the content is "about" and the "point" of it can be confusing when reading difficult information.

Examples of About-Point:

Social Studies: This section is about <u>the military strategy of the Revolutionary War,</u> and the point is <u>that the colonies used unconventional methods of warfare.</u>

Math: This section is about <u>fractions,</u> and the point is <u>that fractions show a part of the whole.</u>

Science: This section is about <u>water pollution,</u> and the point is that <u>many people in poor countries die from drinking contaminated water.</u>

Procedure

1. Before beginning the lesson write the pattern below on the board or overhead. (You can use a transparency of page 33.)
   This section is about _____,
   and the point is _____.
   You may want to highlight or write the words *about* and *point* in a different color.

2. Ask students to read the first paragraph or small subsection of a text. (Read this aloud for beginning ELLs.)

3. Write three possible "about" statements on the board or overhead. Ask students to decide which is the best "about" statement. Students should discuss and support their answers. Fill in the pattern sentence with the "about" statement that was chosen as the best.

4. Next, write three "point" statements on the board or overhead. Ask students to identify the best "point" statement. Students should discuss and support their answers. Fill in the pattern sentence with the "point"

ENGLISH LANGUAGE LEVEL

Speech Emergence to Proficiency

KEY VOCABULARY

- about
- point

Define *about* as a category or item. Define *point* as what the author wants readers to know about the category or item.

RESEARCH BASE

Martin, Lorton, Blanc, & Evans (1977)

Initially ELLs may have difficulty participating in this strategy in a whole-class setting. However, it is important for them to see this strategy modeled. Later, it can be reinforced in small group setting.

that was chosen as the best.

5. Ask students to read a second selection of text.

6. Next, ask them to share and discuss what might be a good "about" statement for this selection. After a statement has been decided upon, write it on the board or overhead.

7. Follow the above procedure for the accompanying "point" statement. Write it on the board or overhead.

8. Ask students to read a third paragraph and work with a partner or in a triad to develop "about" and "point" statements.

9. Write the statements developed by the groups on the board or overhead. Discuss. Ask students to silently read the rest of the selection and independently write their own "about-point" suggestions for each paragraph or selected subsections.

■ ■ ■ ■ ■ ■ ■ ■ ■ Extensions ■ ■ ■ ■ ■ ■ ■ ■ ■

■ Assign specific paragraphs to certain students and ask them to develop "about-point" statements for that paragraph. Discuss as a class.

■ Use "about-point" statements as a homework activity. Assign a section of text to be read and ask students to develop "about-point" statements.

■ Compile a list of student-generated "about-point" statements for a large portion of text. Students can then use these as a study guide and test review.

Sample Progress Indicators for
ABOUT-POINT

Student will:	A	IP	Notes
Participate in whole group, pair, or triad discussions.			
Compare and contrast information.			
Defend or support a statement.			
Analyze and synthesize information.			
Listen to and respond to the work of others.			
Write about subject matter information.			

Metacognitive Strategies

About-Point Activity Sheet

Text: _____

Page: _____   **Paragraph or Section:** _____

This section is **about** _____,

and the **point** is _____

_____.

Text: _____

Page: _____   **Paragraph or Section:** _____

This section is **about** _____,

and the **point** is _____

_____.

Text: _____

Page: _____   **Paragraph or Section:** _____

This section is **about** _____,

and the **point** is _____

_____.

Text: _____

Page: _____   **Paragraph or Section:** _____

This section is **about** _____,

and the **point** is _____

_____.

Comprehension Strategies for English Language Learners   Scholastic Teaching Resources

Think Alouds

ENGLISH LANGUAGE LEVEL

Speech Emergence to
Proficiency

KEY VOCABULARY
- think
- aloud

RESEARCH BASE

Baumann, J.F., Seifert-
Kessell, N., & Jones, L.A.
(1992)

Purpose   This strategy teaches students to monitor their own thinking and understanding by following along as you model strategic thinking through difficult text or problems. It teaches the student to actively choose alternative strategies when something does not make sense.

Key Benefits for ELLs   Having a teacher model what strategic thinkers/readers do to monitor their understanding is particularly helpful for ELLs who are learning a new language and new content simultaneously and need the extra support. In addition, Think Alouds are versatile and can be applied to numerous learning tasks and varied content areas. This enables ELLs to transfer strategic thinking skills to other learning situations.

Procedure

1. Assign a specific task or reading selection. The nature of the think aloud will vary according to the task and content you are teaching.

2. Model how you arrived at the answer or accomplished the task by modeling your thinking "out loud." Go through a step-by-step process of the strategies you are following. For example, clarify the problem by identifying what the task is asking you to accomplish. Discuss what prior knowledge or experiences you might have that relate to the task. Suggest what strategies might be helpful in this learning situation. In addition, monitor your comprehension as you go along. "Is this strategy working for me?" (See the example below.)

3. After the modeling, assign small groups of students to do a task and take turns "thinking aloud."

Example: Science

To compare and contrast the processes of photosynthesis and respiration

CLARIFY THE PROBLEM.   Say: "This task is asking me to compare the processes of photosynthesis and respiration."

ACTIVATE PRIOR KNOWLEDGE.   Continue: "I already know that in respiration carbon dioxide is given off, and in photosynthesis oxygen is given off. They seem to be the opposite of each other."

CHOOSE A STRATEGY.   Suggest: "Maybe I'll use a T-chart or other graphic organizer to compare and contrast the similarities and differences. It may be a good idea to write both formulas and begin by comparing those." *(Demonstrate the strategy.)*

MONITOR COMPREHENSION.   Follow up: "I think this is working. I can see the similarities and differences now between the two processes."

Example: Math

To reduce a fraction to a mixed number.

CLARIFY THE PROBLEM. Say: "Let's see. This problem is asking me to reduce this fraction to a mixed number."

ACTIVATE PRIOR KNOWLEDGE. Continue: "I know that a mixed number contains a whole number and I am going to have to divide in order to reduce the fraction. I'm not sure which number is the divisor."

CHOOSE A STRATEGY. Suggest: "Maybe I'll go back into the chapter and review the example problems for mixed numbers. Then I'll use these numbers in the process and see what I get." *(Demonstrates the strategy.)*

MONITOR COMPREHENSION. Follow up: "These examples seem to fit the problem and when I divide the numerator by the denominator, I get a whole number and a fraction. This seems to be correct. Maybe I'll ask others what they think."

> It is effective to use think alouds when explaining to ELLs the process used to solve story problems.

■ ■ ■ ■ ■ ■ ■ ■ Extensions ■ ■ ■ ■ ■ ■ ■ ■ ■

- For ELLs: Ask students to share the strategies they used when learning in their first language or in a prior school experience. Ask them to share with the class in the form of a think aloud.

- Have students work in pairs to solve a problem using the think aloud strategy. Each student models his or her think aloud strategy to a partner.

Sample Progress Indicators for
THINK ALOUD

Student will:	A	IP	Notes
Verbalize relationships between new information and information previously learned.			
Verbalize the use of strategic strategies for self-monitoring comprehension.			
Evaluate his or her own success in a completed task.			
Imitate the behaviors of native English speakers to complete tasks successfully.			

QAR: Question-Answer Relationships

ENGLISH LANGUAGE LEVEL

Speech Emergence to Proficiency

KEY VOCABULARY
- author
- head
- text

Be sure ELLs understand that the word *head* as it is used in this strategy means "mind."

RESEARCH BASE

Raphael, T. (1986)

Purpose   QAR strategy teaches students that there are two broad sources of information for answering questions: the text and their own background knowledge.

Key Benefits for ELLs   Understanding questions and how to formulate answers can be a challenge for ELLs. QAR is a strategy that can aid ELLs in categorizing and understanding questions and thus lead to a more successful outcome for an answer.

Background   QAR divides questions and responses into two broad categories: In the Text and In My Head. These two categories are then each subdivided into two components, as shown and explained below.

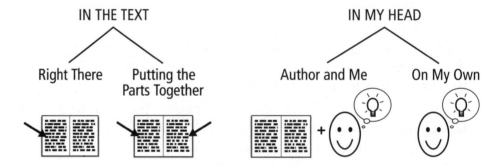

IN THE TEXT		IN MY HEAD	
Right There	Putting the Parts Together	Author and Me	On My Own

IN THE TEXT: This information (answers) is found written in the passage or text.

Right There: This information that can be found in a single sentence or with another connecting sentence.

Putting the Parts Together: This information is found in various parts of the passage, perhaps in two separate paragraphs. It is often associated with these types of questions: compare/contrast, cause/effect, list/example, problem/solution.

IN MY HEAD: These questions and answers involve thinking on the part of students.

Author and Me: The information is found in the written text and from readers' background knowledge. These questions would make no sense to readers unless they read the text. For example, if the class read about the Revolutionary War and the winter at Valley Forge, you might ask, "How do you think the soldiers at Valley Forge were feeling?" A student might respond, "Discouraged, afraid, sick." The student would have read the text explaining the hardships and then interject how the soldiers might be responding to the situation based upon his or her background knowledge of how a person might respond when faced with these challenges.

On My Own: This information must come from readers' personal knowledge or background knowledge. It will not be found in the text. Opinion questions are an example.

Procedure

1. Read a sample text from the overhead or write it on the board or on chart paper. A copy may be given to students. (See sample text and questions on page 38.)

2. After the text (passage) is read, generate questions that fall into each of the QAR question categories (Right There, Putting the Parts Together, Author and Me, On My Own).

   Example of a Right There Question:
   - Read the first question.
   - Ask a student to respond.
   - Then ask, "How do you know?"
   - The student replies, "Because it says so in the story."
   - Ask him or her to point where the answer is written in the text and read.
   - Then relate the answer to the correct QAR category and explain the concept.

3. Then continue with the rest of the questions and answers, relating them to the QAR strategy.

4. Copy and use the QAR cards (page 39) for group responses. Students can point to or hold up the appropriate card when asked to identify the type of Question-Answer Relationships required.

Sample Progress Indicators for
QAR: QUESTION-ANSWER RELATIONSHIP

Student will:	A	IP	Notes
Select, connect, and explain information.			
Use context to construct meaning.			
Provide clarification.			
Understand and identify question type.			
Locate and verbally explain answers to questions.			

Sample QAR Passage and Questions

> ## Jack's Busy Day
>
> Jack woke up early. He ate breakfast and took out the garbage.
>
> Then he went to the garage and washed and waxed his new sports car. He listened to rock music while he cleaned the inside of the car.
>
> He was glad when Mother called him in for lunch.

Questions:

1. What did Jack do while he listened to rock music?

Answer: He cleaned the inside of his car.
QAR type: Right There

2. What tasks did Jack do before lunchtime?

Answer: He ate breakfast, took out the garbage, washed and waxed his car, and cleaned the inside of his car.
QAR type: Putting the Parts Together

3. Explain how you wash a car.

Answer: Individual answers will vary.
QAR type: On My Own

4. Why was Jack glad to hear it was lunchtime?

Answer: Answers will vary.
Example: Because he had worked hard and was hungry.
QAR type: Author and Me

Comprehension Strategies for English Language Learners   Scholastic Teaching Resources

Metacognitive Strategies

QAR Cards

Right There

Putting the Parts Together

Author and Me

On My Own

GIST: Generating Interaction Between Schemata and Text

ENGLISH LANGUAGE LEVEL

Speech Emergence to Proficiency

KEY VOCABULARY

- details
- gist
- important
- repeated
- summary
- topic sentence
- unimportant

RESEARCH BASE

Cunningham, J. (1982)

Muth & Alvermann, (1999)

Purpose   GIST provides an opportunity for students to identify important vocabulary and synthesize important pieces of information into summary statement to show the gist of the reading. It facilitates understanding how the "parts" fit together to make the "whole." This strategy also shows them how to distinguish between important and less important pieces of information and how to group similar ideas together.

Key Benefits for ELLs   The process of summarization can greatly assist ELLs in comprehending expository text. When faced with reading an extended text that contains a multitude of information, they can be overwhelmed with information and at a loss as to how to recognize important information from varying degrees of details. In this strategy, students work collaboratively to decide upon the important information included in a specific selection of text and use it to write a summary statement. This procedure is repeated until an expanded section of text is summarized. A comprehensive summary statement/paragraph is then written. This strategy also provides ELLs with an opportunity to verbally discuss the content material and vocabulary and clarify meaning.

Procedure

1. Prepare a transparency of a section of text or designates a portion of text to be read. This usually includes text that may be a challenge for the students.

2. Typically, in a class of all native English speakers, you and students read the section silently. For ELLs, it is more effective if you read the passage aloud while they follow along.

> The original strategy has been adapted somewhat to take into consideration the needs of ELLs. It is particularly helpful for you to model the strategy initially and explain the process.

3. As a class, decide upon the "most important" words or concepts that are essential to understanding that portion of the text. (The number of concepts and words may vary depending upon the length of the text.) You can underline or highlight these on the overhead. (It is helpful for students to have a copy of the text so they can underline also.) You can also ask ELLs to write the words and concepts on the GIST Activity Sheet (page 43).

4. Using as many of the "most important words and concepts" as possible, write a summary statement consisting of one or two sentences together with students. These sentences should offer the "gist" of the reading passage.

5. Each student then writes the completed summary statement on the GIST Activity Sheet.

6. Repeat the procedure using subsequent sections of the text.

7. Finally, students use the summary statements that have already been generated as a comprehensive summary for the entire text. These can be grouped together to form a summary paragraph.

Working in Cooperative Groups

After students are familiar with the process, this should be done as a *cooperative group strategy*. Follow these steps:

1. Assign a section of text for students to read.
2. Form groups and assign a group leader.
3. Students read the text silently (or a group member can read it aloud).
4. The group collaboratively identifies important vocabulary and concepts.
5. The group develops the summary statement identifying the gist of the reading.
6. Each member of the group writes the summary statement on a piece of paper.
7. The group reads the next portion of text and repeats the process.
8. Move from group to group observing and providing support when needed.
9. Each group presents its summary statement(s).
10. Discuss as a class and compare.

> For this activity, it is helpful to place ELLs in groups with strong English speakers and readers. If a beginning level ELL is included in the group, try to place this student with a student who speaks the same language. If needed, first language support can be offered.

Sample Paragraph (With Important Words/Concepts Identified)

Twenty-five years ago, India was experiencing a hunger crisis. Many people predicted a bleak future for this country's people. However, India now produces enough food for its entire country because its government spent so much time on farm and economic planning. India still has problems—many undernourished people and a high infant death rate—but overall much progress has been made.

Summary Statement: In the past, India's people suffered from hunger, but now because of government planning, India produces enough food to feed the entire country.

■ ■ ■ ■ ■ ■ ■ ■ Extensions ■ ■ ■ ■ ■ ■ ■ ■ ■

When ELLs become more comfortable working in cooperative groups, you can have each group be responsible for summarizing a different section of text. Discuss the varying summary statements and write them on the board. Then students can copy them to use as study guides. Students might also explain how they constructed their summary.

Sample Progress Indicators for GIST

Student will:	A	IP	Notes
Work collaboratively to identify key content vocabulary and important ideas in a specific section of text.			
Write summary sentences of selected text.			
Combine summary sentences to write a comprehensive summary of a longer section of text.			
Orally present a summary statement(s) developed by the group.			

Metacognitive Strategies

GIST Activity Sheet

Directions: Read to the summary point. Next, identify the important vocabulary or concepts. Then write a summary statement explaining the "gist" of the reading.

Summary point: _____

Important words or concepts: _____

_____

_____

↓

Summary statement (gist): _____

_____

_____

_____

_____

Summary point:

Important words or concepts:

_____

_____

↓

Summary statement (gist):

_____

_____

_____

_____

Comprehension Strategies for English Language Learners   Scholastic Teaching Resources

Reading Guide-O-Rama

RESEARCH BASE

Cunningham R. & Shablak, S. (1975)

Tierney, R., Readence, J.E., & Dishner, E.K. (1985)

Purpose   The purpose of a reading guide is to provide you with an opportunity to give students an idea of how to obtain information through text. Through the reading guide, you are able to give "expert" guidance to students as to the most productive way to read and think about a specific content reading assignment. Reading guides point out important information as well as unimportant information and help the student selectively read text. This strategy can be used for any content subject reading assignment.

Key Benefits for ELLs   The content teacher is the "expert" at modeling how to glean specific information from text. Often content text is so rich in detail that sorting through these details can be a daunting task for ELLs. Reading guides provide a form of scaffolding between student readers, a teacher's specific purposes, and the content text. This particular tool is very valuable for ELLs, who must tackle the challenges of new content language but also decide what is important and unimportant to the purposes of the assignment.

> Constructing reading guides can become a department or content team project. It is a time-saver to share the writing of reading guides by dividing the assignments among colleagues. Everyone can then share the various guides.

Procedure

1. Determine the purpose for a specific reading assignment.
2. Decide how you as an "expert" reader would approach this reading task.
3. Choose which parts of the text are important or unimportant to understanding the purpose of the assignment.
4. Decide, step-by-step, what reading behaviors students should use to understand the specific purpose of the reading assignment.
5. Construct a Reading Guide-O-Rama for students to use while reading the text selection.

Example: History Reading Guide-O-Rama

Page 26: Read the title and first heading in the chapter. What do you think it will be about? Write down your ideas. Be prepared to go back and check your predictions.

Page 26, paragraphs 2–5: Reread the first paragraph on page 24. Then carefully read this section. How did the strategy of the Continental army change? We will discuss your ideas in class.

Page 28, paragraphs 3 and 4: This information is not necessary for our purposes. Skim or skip this part.

Page 30, column 1: This column gives a summary of why the battle of Saratoga was the turning point of the Revolutionary War. Before you read further be sure you understand the reasons. If you do not understand, reread this part. If you still have questions ask me for help.

Page 32, column 2: This column describes Washington's trip across the Delaware River. Read the information and then draw a picture of this event.

Example: Science Reading Guide-O-Rama

Page 110, paragraph 1 and 2: Read this section quickly to get an idea of what the chapter is about.

Page 111, paragraph 3: Read this paragraph carefully. It explains the graph on page 112. After you read the paragraph, look at the graph. In your own words explain the information it gives you.

Page 113, column 2: Read these instructions carefully. Discuss with your lab partner how you will conduct this experiment. Write down your plans and then discuss them with me before you begin.

Leveled Reading Guide-O-Rama

Students bring to the classroom diverse language needs and competencies. A leveled reading guide allows the teacher to choose which questions and tasks students are to attempt. The items on the reading guide can be marked with asterisks and leveled according to difficulty. For example:

   * *All* students are to complete:
   ** *Group 1* students are to complete:
   *** *Group 2* students are to complete:

Sample Progress Indicators for
READING GUIDE-O-RAMA

Student will:	A	IP	Notes
Follow written directions included in the reading guide.			
Focus attention selectively within the reading assignment.			
Demonstrate the use of varying reading strategies.			
Monitor his or her comprehension.			

Question Guides

Purpose The purpose of this strategy is to give students a purpose for reading and direct their attention to the information that is targeted by the questions in a teacher-prepared guide.

Key Benefits for ELLs It is often very challenging for ELLs to have to read and evaluate text information at the same time. Also, it can be very difficult for them to decipher what is essential information and what is nonessential information. In addition, initially stating a purpose for reading helps students understand the objective of the lesson. This strategy allows you to guide the students' reading by assigning specific sections of text for them to read and asking questions that focus upon the purpose and intent of the assignment. Material that might be included on a test can be incorporated into the question guide. Strategies such as the ones exhibited on the Question Guide provide a structured framework from which ELLs can build specific content knowledge.

Procedure

1. Construct a question guide that sets a purpose for reading. Explain what you want students to accomplish by reading the text and completing the question guide.

> A completed question guide can serve as an excellent tool for review for ELLS.

2. Assign specific sections of text to be read and develop corresponding questions. These should support the purpose for reading.

3. Use the reproducible Question Guide form (page 48) and review the model (page 47) to help you create guides for your classroom.

Question Guide

Topic: Photosynthesis

Purpose: The main purpose of this reading assignment is for you to recognize the most important steps in the process of photosynthesis. You should also know how light, water, and carbon dioxide combine to form sugar. In addition, you should gain insight into the complexity of the process.

Directions: Read only the parts that are listed in the reading directions. After you read a specific part, respond to the questions.

Reading Directions	Questions
1. Page 70, paragraphs 1, 2, and 3. Then answer the questions.	Define the word photosynthesis by its parts. What does it mean? In what part of the plant does photosynthesis take place? How does the waxy coating on leaves help protect the inner part?
2. Page 71, paragraphs 3 and 4. Then answer the questions.	What is a chloroplast? What makes chloroplasts green?
3. Page 72, Read paragraphs 1, 2, 3, and 4. Read the graph at the bottom of the page.	What are the five steps in photosynthesis? 1. 2. 3. 4. 5. What is the equation that shows photosynthesis? Write it here.
4. Read the questions first. Then read page 73, paragraph 2.	How is the word respiration used in this paragraph? How is it related to energy?

> You may want to have students answer the questions on a separate sheet of paper.

Sample Progress Indicators for
QUESTION GUIDE

Student will:	A	IP	Notes
Follow written directions.			
Read and focus attention selectively.			
Respond to written questions.			
Understand purpose for reading.			
Locate specific information.			

Question Guide

Topic: _____

Purpose: _____

_____

_____

_____

_____

Directions: Read only the parts that are listed in the reading directions. After you read a specific part, respond to the questions.

Reading Directions	Questions

Comprehension Strategies for English Language Learners Scholastic Teaching Resources

Previewing Text

Purpose   The purpose of previewing text is to teach students to generate questions and set purposes that will lead to more-proficient processing of information. It enables them to develop a sense of what a text or chapter selection is about before actually reading it. Students learn to monitor their comprehension and gain more independence in a reading situation. When students generate questions about the content material they are previewing, they generally seek the answers in their reading. Therefore, students become more involved and active during the reading process.

Key Benefits for ELLs   For ELLs, previewing text is a way to set a framework for understanding the content of a text and helps them distinguish between important and irrelevant information.

Procedure

1. Prepare overheads of several pages of the material to be previewed. You can use a transparency of the worksheet and complete it as a whole-class activity.

2. Guide students through a step-by-step preview of the text:
   Example:

   - First, read the title and convert it to a question. Explain to students that they can access prior knowledge to help them generate a question.

     Title of Chapter: "The Oil Boom"
       Preview Questions: What does *boom* mean here?
                                     How is that related to oil?

   - Next, read the introduction and summary and questions. Ask, *What are the author's main points?* Point out the significant verbal cues and their meanings such as *such as, for example, for instance, most important, in conclusion, therefore.* This is particularly helpful for ELLs.

   - Read the headings and subheadings. Convert these to questions. For example:

     Heading: Drilling for Oil
       Preview Questions: How do you drill for oil?
                                     Does it really gush out of the ground?
     Subheading: The Natural Gas Bonus
       Preview Questions: What is natural gas?
                                     Is natural gas the same thing as oil?

ENGLISH LANGUAGE LEVEL
Speech Emergence to Proficiency

KEY VOCABULARY
- preview
- summary

RESEARCH BASE
Dole, J.A., Valencia, S.W., Greer, E.A., & Wardrop, J.L. (1991)

Meyer, B.J., Brandt, K.M., & Bluth, G.J. (1980)

Pressley, M., Almasi, J., Schuder, T., Bergman, J., Hite, S., El-Dinary, P.B., & Brown, R. (1992)

- Continue by reading and emphasizing the print in different fonts and special effects, such as boldface, italics, color, captions, and word bubbles. Let students know that these features signal important information or key vocabulary.

  Preview Question: Why are certain words, phrases, or sentences written in this way?

- Finally, discuss the illustrations, photographs, and the captions with each, as well as the graphic organizers that might include diagrams, cross sections, overlays, maps, tables, charts, graphs, and framed text.

  Preview Question: What do these graphics tell you about the chapter's content?

3. Give students a copy of the Text Preview sheet (page 51). Ask them to open their books to another part of the chapter and preview this section using the guidelines delineated on the worksheet. When students have completed their sheet, ask for volunteers to share their results and discuss as a class.

> Consider asking ELLs to complete a Text Preview sheet before beginning new sections of text or a reading assignment at home.

Text Organizers

At the beginning of the school year, as a whole-class activity, preview the content classroom textbook and explain the text organizers. These include Table of Contents, Glossary, Index, Preface, Appendix, and References. Many times, ELLs may not have had exposure to American textbooks. Understanding text organizers and how to use them can save much time for both students and the teacher.

The following list describes how each element identifies text:

Titles, headings, and subheadings . . . . .ranks ideas

Boldface, italics, color, underlining . . . . .highlights

Captions for pictures, illustrations . . . . .explains

Graphics and visual aids . . . . .explains

Questions . . . . .sets purpose

Glossary, footnotes, appendix, references . . . . .defines or explains

Sample Progress Indicators for
PREVIEWING TEXT

Student will:	A	IP	Notes
Understand and use textual cues.			
Understand and use visual aids.			
Understand and use textual organizers.			
Generate questions while previewing text.			
Preview text before reading an assignment.			

Text Preview

Directions: Follow these guidelines and preview the assigned text.

Assignment: _____

1. Read the title. Create a question using the title. _____

   _____

2. Read the introduction, summary, and questions. What are the author's main

   points? _____

   _____

   _____

3. Read the headings and subheadings. Create questions from them.

   _____

   _____

   _____

4. What print is in boldface, italics, color, captions, or word bubbles?

   _____

   _____

5. Look at the illustrations and pictures. What do they tell you about the

   content? _____

   _____

   _____

   _____

6. Look at the graphs, diagrams, maps, tables, charts, overlays, and framed text.

   What do they tell you about the content? _____

   _____

   _____

   _____

Comprehension Strategies for English Language Learners   Scholastic Teaching Resources

Coding Text

ENGLISH LANGUAGE LEVEL

Speech Emergence to Proficiency

KEY VOCABULARY
- code
- means
- "stands for"
- sticky note

RESEARCH BASE

Alvermann, D.E. (1982)

Armbruster, B.B. & Anderson, T.H. (1981)

Kulhavy, R.W., Dyer, J.W., & Silver, L. (1975)

Purpose   Coding text is a form of annotation that allows students to monitor their comprehension while reading.

Key Benefits for ELLs   Coding text gives students a method to react to text and express their thinking while reading. It helps ELLs to identify unknown language or concepts. Often by the time the text is completely read, students have forgotten what areas might have been challenging or what the important points were. Therefore, it is a helpful tool in aiding ELLs to identify and remember important information or challenging words/concepts.

After learning the coding strategy, students may want to devise their own personal system. Provide an opportunity for them to brainstorm codes with you.

Sample codes:
I or **!** for important
C or **?** for confusing
U or **draw a circle** around an unknown word or term
PK or ***** for prior knowledge (students can relate to previous knowledge). This is particularly significant for ELLs who may have covered the content in their native country.

Procedure

1. The most effective way to teach coding is to model it on an overhead projector. Use a think aloud format. Choose a uniform code with a few possibilities. Starting with too many codes may cause confusion.

2. Copy a section of text to show on the overhead.

3. Give each student a copy of the text.

4. Read the text aloud and model "thinking" while reading. For example, pretend to come across an unknown word and mark it with the correct code. Continue this for other areas such as important facts or ideas, confusing concepts, and so on.

5. Ask students to read the text and code it accordingly.

6. After they are finished coding the text, discuss the results and answer questions.

Using Sticky Notes to Code Text

When students are not allowed to write in textbooks, use sticky notes to mark text. Sticky notes are a wonderful alternative because they help students attend to a task and become actively involved. Model this process using the following steps:

1. Select a portion of text from the textbook.

2. Read aloud as students follow along.

3. Demonstrate how to write the code on a sticky note and place it by the correct portion of text. For example, an unknown word can be written on the sticky note with the correct code and placed by the section of text where it is found.

4. Distribute sticky notes to students. Ask them to read a portion of text and mark it as necessary using sticky notes.

5. After reading, discuss the outcomes.

Using Sticky Notes With Content Vocabulary

Using sticky notes with a focus on vocabulary helps students see key words in context. Follow these steps:

1. Write vocabulary words or other terms on sticky notes.

2. Say the word to students and explain its meaning.

3. Have students locate the word in the text and place a sticky note beside it.

4. You can also incorporate illustrations in the text. For example, if the term is "American flag," students search the text and locate a picture of the American flag, placing a sticky note on or near it.

Sample Progress Indicators for
CODING TEXT

Student will:	A	IP	Notes
Use a coding system to mark text.			
Use the code to aid in comprehension.			
Develop a personal coding system.			

Herringbone Technique

ENGLISH LANGUAGE LEVEL

Speech Emergence to Proficiency

KEY VOCABULARY

- who
- what
- when
- where
- why
- how
- detail
- main idea
- support

RESEARCH BASE

Tierney, Readence, & Dishner (1985)

Purpose   This graphic organizer supports comprehension of text by providing a framework upon which the *who, what, when, why, where,* and *how* questions can be visually organized in relation to the main idea.

Key Benefits for ELLs   Being able to answer and understand the questions *who, what, when, why, where,* and *how* can greatly aid ELLs when reading and comprehending text. This strategy also shows the relationship of the details to the main idea, which is often a troublesome concept for ELLs. This strategy is particularly well suited for expository text but can also be used with narrative text.

Procedure

1. Select a text for students to read.

   Example:

   The Growth of Factories in the Northeast

   Samuel Slater worked in the mills of England for seven years. He knew how to build cotton-spinning machines and how to use water to power them. In 1789, he boarded a ship for the United States. Slater located a spot to build a mill along the Blackstone River in Rhode Island. Most people spun yarn by hand, which was a slow process. Slater's mill had water-powered machines that spun yarn quickly. This made the cost of yarn lower.

2. Draw a diagram of the herringbone on the board or overhead. (You can also use a copy of the activity sheet, page 56).

   Example:

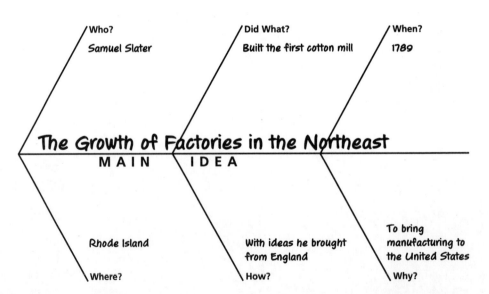

3. Discuss how the smaller bones (details) are attached to the backbone (main idea) of the fish, which serves as the foundation. Then explain how they all work together to provide structure (comprehension) to the whole body (text).

4. Explain to students that they will be asked to look for information that answers the following questions:

    Who is the text talking about?

    What did they do?

    When did they do it?

    Where did they do it?

    How did they do it?

    Why did they do it?

5. Allow time for students to read the text.

6. Give them copies of the diagram and ask them to record the answers to the questions on it. This can be done as a whole-class discussion activity.

7. Show students how the information is organized around a main idea.

8. Using the information on the diagram, students formulate a main idea. The main idea is written on the diagram.

9. After the students learn the procedure, they can complete the diagram on their own. This can then be used as a basis for comparison and class discussion. It can also serve as a springboard to writing.

10. The strategy can be reversed and students can first formulate the main idea and then identify the supporting details.

■ ■ ■ ■ ■ ■ ■ ■ ■ ■ Extensions ■ ■ ■ ■ ■ ■ ■ ■ ■ ■

■ Assign the students to teams. Each team is responsible for completing a herringbone diagram for a specific assignment. Each team then shares with the class the results of its herringbone diagram. The results of each team are compared and contrasted.

■ Students can use the herringbone strategy to help them organize information and write a summary paragraph.

Sample Progress Indicators for
HERRINGBONE TECHNIQUE

Student will:	A	IP	Notes
Synthesize, analyze, and infer from information.			
Represent information visually.			
Formulate a main idea.			
Connect information to the main idea.			
Answer questions.			

Herringbone Technique

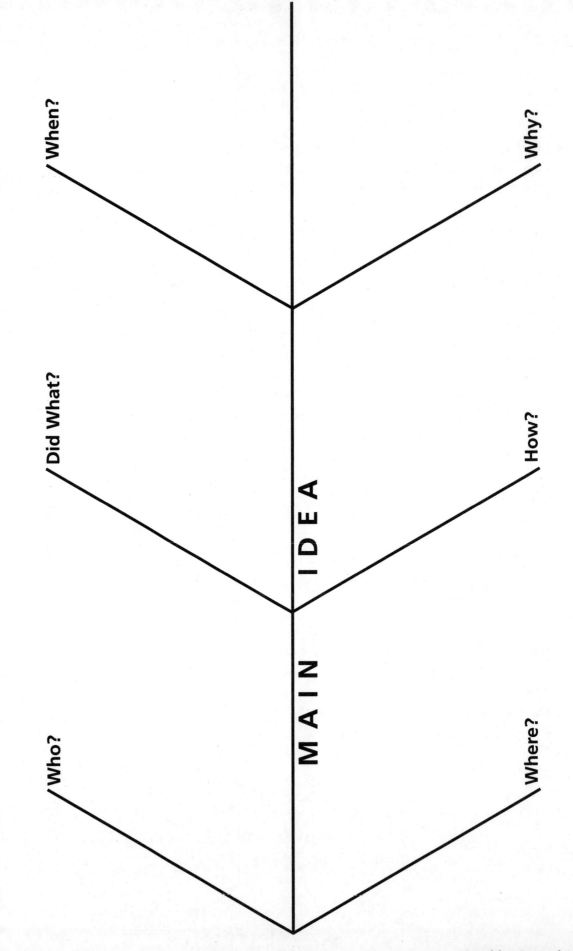

When?

Did What?

Who?

MAIN IDEA

Why?

How?

Where?

Comprehension Strategies for English Language Learners Scholastic Teaching Resources

Opinion-Proof

Purpose   The purpose of Opinion-Proof is to provide a framework for students to develop and organize opinions and transform these opinions into persuasive speaking and writing. Opinion-Proof also requires students to use higher-order literacy skills including evaluation, verification, and persuasion.

Key Benefits for ELLs   It is very important that ELLs engage in the practice of higher-order literacy skills. This includes the writing process, which can be a challenge for ELLs. In addition, distinguishing between fact and opinion and being able to support that opinion are essential literacy skills. Opinion-Proof requires the student to form an opinion (evaluative), support the opinion (verify), and write convincingly about their opinion (persuasion). In addition, during the peer-editing process, students develop criteria upon which to evaluate their writing, react to the writing of others, receive the opinion of others, and revise their own writing. If the process is paired with "framed paragraphs," students can work from a basic framework and begin the process of persuasive thinking and writing. This is very helpful to students who are in the beginning stages of learning the "how to" of effective writing. This strategy also provides an opportunity for ELLs to evaluate their own work, share it with a classmate (peer editing), and then revise the paragraph before submitting a final draft.

ENGLISH LANGUAGE LEVEL

Early production to Proficiency

KEY VOCABULARY

- evidence
- opinion
- proof
- prove

RESEARCH BASE

Santa, C., Dudley, S.C., & Nelson, M. (1985)

Procedure

1. Choose a portion of text to be read silently from which an opinion will be solicited. (This can be used in many content areas.)

2. Give students a copy of the Opinion-Proof Framework Sheet (see page 59) or write it on the board.

3. Ask students to write an opinion and support it with evidence from the text.

    Example:

Opinion Statement	Evidence to Prove My Opinion
Sacagawea was an important member of the Corps of Discovery.	She was an excellent navigator.
	Since she knew several languages, she could act as a translator.
	Her presence among the corps symbolized peace to the Indians they met.
	Meeting her long-lost brother helped the corps get horses and other important items.

4. Ask students to write a paragraph using their opinion as the topic sentence. The evidence is used as supporting details for the opinion statement. You can use a "framed paragraph" to provide a framework and transition from information to writing the paragraph.

Example: "framed paragraph"

Sacagawea was an _____ part of the Corps of Discovery. One reason I feel this way is because _____. In addition, _____. Also, _____. Finally, _____

Example: completed "framed paragraph"

Sacagawea was an important member of the Corps of Discovery. One reason I feel this way is because she was such an excellent navigator. In addition, her role as translator was very helpful. Also, she was seen as a symbol of peace to other Indians the corps met. Finally, meeting her long-lost brother helped the corps get horses and other important items.

Peer Editing

- Students develop criteria for judging their writing, such as, "Does my paragraph state my opinion as the main idea?" "Do I have enough supporting evidence?" "Does each sentence support the main idea?"
- Students divide into pairs and read and respond to each other's writing.
- Students revise their paragraphs based upon the input given. Students then turn in a final draft of the paragraph.

Sample Progress Indicators for OPINION-PROOF

Student will:	A	IP	Notes
Develop an opinion and write it as a statement.			
Support opinion with evidence.			
Write a persuasive paragraph.			
React to the work of others (verbally).			
Revise own writing based upon peer input.			

Cognitive Strategies

Opinion-Proof Framework Sheet

Opinion Statement	Evidence to Prove My Opinion

Framed Paragraph:

OPINION STATEMENT

One reason I feel this way is because

In addition,

Also,

Finally,

Semantic Feature Analysis

RESEARCH BASE

Anders, P.L., & Bos, C.S. (1986)

Johnson, D., Toms-Bronowski, S., & Pittleman, S.D. (1986)

Purpose   The purpose of semantic feature analysis (also called attribute charting) is to give students an opportunity to construct a visual representation that identifies a specific members of a category or concept by analyzing and defining their characteristics.

Key Benefits for ELLs   Information presented in textbooks generally abounds with abstract concepts along with relationships to subordinate concepts and features. Often, identifying these relationships is difficult for ELLs. Semantic feature analysis is beneficial for ELLs because it offers them an opportunity to create a visual representation of new terms or concepts and connect them to other related terms. This strategy is helpful in clarifying abstract relationships among complicated concepts. In addition, this strategy is excellent for delineating frequently confused terms. As they construct a semantic feature chart, ELLs have the opportunity to actively investigate and define concepts. This strategy aids students in keeping the information in long-term memory.

Procedure

1. Choose the main concept and subordinate concepts or categories within it that you expect students to learn and understand. For example, Main category (concept): Means of air travel.

   Suggested topics:

   History: events, people

   Geography: natural resources, topography

   Math: properties of numbers, processes

   Science: properties of various substances, chemical reactions.

2. Identify members of the main category: Members: biplane, propeller plane, jet, supersonic, space shuttle, helicopter, seaplane.

3. Identify the critical features of the category, such as water, space, propeller, jet engine, faster than speed of sound, public. You may also introduce the main concept, then through whole-class discussion tap into the students' prior knowledge and together generate members of the category and features.

4. Create a chart and give each student a copy (see page 62). Discuss the items on the chart depicting the main category, subordinate categories, and features.

Example:

Means of Air Travel

	Water	Space	Propeller	Faster Than the Speed of Sound	Public
biplane	–	–	+	–	
propeller plane	–	–	+	–	+
jet	–	–	–	–	+
supersonic jet	–		–	+	+
space shuttle		+	–	+	–
seaplane	+	–	+	–	+

+ Yes, it has this feature.   **–** No, it does not have this feature.

5. Explain to students how to complete the chart. You may want to use a plus sign or a minus sign to indicate the relationship (see above). You may also wish to use other symbols. If students are using the Semantic Feature Analysis Chart while reading or conducting an investigation, the addition of a question mark may be useful. When students become familiar with the strategy, a numerical system can be used, such as 0 = none, 1 = some, 2 = much, 3 = all.

6. When students understand the process, ask them to complete the chart by conducting their own research. You may also conduct a whole-class activity, with the entire class participating in making predictions. Students then mark the chart in pencil so that they can a make adjustments when more information is available. Decisions are made by consensus. Ask individual students to make predictions on their charts, read for confirmation, and make any adjustments that are necessary.

7. After students have read or researched the topic, confirm their responses through class discussion or cooperative group discussion. Make any changes to whole-class predictions by mutual agreement.

■ ■ ■ ■ ■ ■ ■ Extensions ■ ■ ■ ■ ■ ■ ■

- Semantic mapping can be a foundation for writing a paper about the topic. For beginning ELLs, use sentence frames, such as:
  1. Supersonic planes and the _space_ _shuttle_ can travel faster than the _speed_ _of_ _sound_ .
  2. A _seaplane_ can land in the water.
- Students can draw and label the members and their features.
- Students can write a paragraph comparing and contrasting some of the members of the category.
- Charts can be used as a study tool for tests.

Sample Progress Indicators for
SEMANTIC FEATURE ANALYSIS

Student will:	A	IP	Notes
Follow oral and written directions.			
Participate in whole-class discussions.			
Make predictions.			
Analyze, compare, and contrast information.			
Represent information visually.			
Understand content concepts and their relationship to one another.			

Semantic Feature Analysis Chart

CATEGORY _____

Features:

Members of Category:						

+ Yes, it has this feature.   **–** No, it does not have this feature.

Cognitive Strategies

Comprehension Strategies for English Language Learners Scholastic Teaching Resources

Guided Imagery

Purpose   The purpose of this strategy is to teach students to create mental images that will produce associations between new concepts or facts being learned and students' prior knowledge. Guided imagery can be used in many curricular areas.

Key Benefits for ELLs   The use of imagery before and during reading can greatly benefit learning and recall of information. According to K.D. Wood (1989), most adolescents do not use imagery spontaneously unless they are taught to do so. For example, after a student has created a mental image, encourage the student to describe it. This provides an opportunity for you to evaluate the student's response and support it or clear up any misunderstandings. This strategy is particularly helpful for English language learners who may have formed mistaken images due to misunderstandings related to language. In addition, guided imagery, when presented orally, focuses attention upon the skill of listening.

Procedure

For expository text, use imagery that illustrates the characteristics of key concepts (Wood, K.D., 1989). For students who are unfamiliar with imaging, it is often beneficial to develop their visualization skills by first asking them to create images of familiar, ordinary objects such as a dog, a tree, or a boat. It is also helpful to model (thinking aloud) how to visualize.

1. Tell students to relax, close their eyes, and form a picture of the chosen word(s) by trying to sense how the object looks, sounds, feels, and smells. Tell students to return (in their minds) to the classroom as soon as their mental journey is done.

2. Ask various students to share their images and highlight the details and discuss the differences between them. If a student is having problems visualizing, ask him or her to create a mental sketch of the object and then actually sketch a picture of the object. Use this to make an analogy between "mental sketching" and "pencil sketching."

3. Move from simple objects to sentences. First use a sentence that is personally relevant such as "A teenager is changing the flat tire."

4. Before responding, ask the students to identify the words in the sentence that are needed to form a mental picture. (e.g., *teenager, changing, flat tire*)

5. Students again close their eyes and form mental images

6. Students then describe their images. Discuss these as a group.

7. You can then move to more content specific material, such as "The tiny nucleus floated around the jellylike cytoplasm." (science) Or "On Christmas Eve, George Washington's boat quietly glided across the

ENGLISH LANGUAGE LEVEL

Speech Emergence to Proficiency

KEY VOCABULARY
- imagine
- relax
- images

any content-specific vocabulary

RESEARCH BASE
Irwin, J. (1991)

Wood, K.D. (1989)

Delaware River" (history).

8. Discuss key words and ask probing questions, such as "What do you see in your minds? What do you feel?"

Using a Textbook and Imaging

After students are comfortable with imaging, you may use longer sections of text.

1. **Before Reading:**
   - Choose a section of text for students to read.
   - Tell students that they are going to make pictures or a "movie" in their minds as they read the passage.
   - Ask the class to select "key" (picturesque) words in the title and describe everything that comes to their minds.
   - Discuss various responses as a class.

2. **During Reading:**
   - Students may work individually, in pairs, or triads. First, they underline or put a check mark over key words in the first section of text (usually indicated by a subheading) and form images from these.
   - Students discuss their images within their group.
   - You may elicit some responses for class discussion.
   - Continue in this manner until the entire passage is read.
   - Students may draw sketches or graphic representations of information, if necessary.

3. **After Reading:**
   - Conduct a whole-class discussion of the content, asking for elaboration and inferred details wherever appropriate.
   - Ask students to identify places in the text where they created a mind picture.
   - Ask them to describe these pictures and identify the words that helped them create images.
   - You may evaluate students by asking them to write about the content covered.

Cognitive Strategies

Possible Ways to Use Imaging in Various Content Areas

Math: Story Problems Ask students to create an image of the problem choosing key words. (Students may draw the problem from their image)

Example:
Maria is 5 feet, 4 inches tall.
Carlos is 4 feet, 10 inches tall.
Lucy is 5 feet tall.
Who is the tallest child?

Students may form mental images of three children and their differing heights from tallest to shortest. Ask probing questions related to size and comparison.

History: Boston Tea Party Students can close their eyes while you read an account of the event or follow the directions for textbook use. Follow up by asking probing questions, such as "Do you hear the creak of the ship and the water splashing against the sides? Can you hear the whispers of the colonists as they tiptoe onto the boat? Can you hear the splash of the tea crates as they are thrown into the water? How are they dressed?"

Science: Amoeba Students can close their eyes and picture the slow movement of an amoeba across the glass slide. Ask probing questions.

Science: Photosynthesis Students create images of water being taken in by the roots of a plant and moving through the xylem to food-making cells. Ask probing questions.

**Sample Progress Indicators for
GUIDED IMAGERY**

Student will:	A	IP	Notes
Create mental images of key concepts.			
Verbally share his or her images.			
Interact with text to create images.			
Listen selectively.			

Anticipation-Reaction Guide

ENGLISH LANGUAGE LEVEL

Speech Emergence to Intermediate Fluency

KEY VOCABULARY

- agree
- disagree

RESEARCH BASE

Dufelmeyer, F.A.; Baum, D.D.; & Merkley, D.J. (1987)

Readence, J.E.; Bean, T.W.; & Baldwin, R.S. (1988)

Purpose   Anticipation-Reaction guides activate prior knowledge of a specific topic by asking students to identify their existing ideas or attitudes. This enables students to become interactive readers. These guides are generally made up of three to five statements that are teacher generated. Students are asked to "agree" or "disagree" with these statements before and then again after reading the selection. Students re-evaluate their responses and explain how their thoughts or ideas have changed as a result of reading the material. A simple way to teach this is "thumbs up" or "thumbs down." Illustrations are included on the activity sheet (page 68).

Key Benefits for ELLs   English language learners bring varied perspectives to the reading situation. This strategy allows them to identify their ideas and see them in relation to information offered in the text. It also allows them an opportunity to discuss these perceptions with others. This strategy is helpful to students who may hold misconceptions regarding a specific concept.

Procedure

Anticipation-Reaction guides can take various forms. They apply to content area and narrative text. (See the examples on page 67.)

1. Begin by identifying three to five major concepts—implicit or explicit.

2. Write a clear, short, declarative sentence for each idea.

3. Give each student a copy of the Anticipation-Reaction Guide. Before reading the selection, students react to the statements and check the appropriate box—Agree/Disagree. Students discuss their reactions and should be prepared to defend them. Students then read the selection. The Anticipation-Reaction Guide is revisited and "After Reading" responses recorded. Students compare their "before" and "after" responses and discuss any changes in ideas or perceptions.

4. After completing this activity in a whole group, it can also be done in a small cooperative group setting.

Examples:

Social Studies

Agree-Disagree: Before and After

Before Reading		Statement	After Reading	
Agree 👍	Disagree 👎		Agree 👍	Disagree 👎
		1. George Washington welcomed black slaves in the Continental Army.		
		2. The Revolutionary War was fought primarily for religious reasons.		
		3. Native Americans fought in the Revolutionary War.		
		4.		
		5.		

Math

Agree-Disagree: Before and After

Before Reading		Statement	After Reading	
Agree 👍	Disagree 👎		Agree 👍	Disagree 👎
		1. A negative number is less than zero.		
		2. Negative numbers multiplied result in positive numbers.		
		3. Negative numbers are part of everyday life.		
		4. Negative numbers are difficult to understand.		
		5.		

Science

Agree-Disagree: Before and After

Before Reading		Statement	After Reading	
Agree 👍	Disagree 👎		Agree 👍	Disagree 👎
		1. All mammals have live births.		
		2. Humans are mammals.		
		3. Some mammals make good pets.		
		4.		
		5.		

Sample Progress Indicators for ANTICIPATION GUIDES

Student will:	A	IP	Notes
Use language to persuade or justify reaction to a statement.			
Use the context of the text to construct meaning.			
Use text to self-correct, if necessary.			
Connect new information to information previously learned.			

Agree-Disagree: Before and After

Before Reading		Statement	After Reading	
Agree 👉	**Disagree** 👎		**Agree** 👉	**Disagree** 👎
		1.		
		2.		
		3.		
		4.		
		5.		

Cognitive Strategies

Comprehension Strategies for English Language Learners   Scholastic Teaching Resources

Mapping

Purpose   Semantic mapping serves as a means to give students a spatial and visual venue in which to organize ideas, show relationships, and retain important information. Mapping can be used before, during, or after reading. Before reading, mapping can activate prior knowledge and set a purpose for reading. During reading, additional concepts can be added to embellish the map. Finally, after reading, the map can be reorganized to show growth in the topic area. It can also be expanded at this time. Maps may be developed using whole-group instruction, in cooperative learning groups, or by an individual student.

Key Benefits for ELLs   This strategy gives ELLs both spatial and visual formats in which to organize and share information. Having both of these venues aids their understanding and also provides an opportunity for the interpretation of information that was read. Maps take many and varied forms. They may be as simple as drawing pictures or copying the headings and subheadings from a chapter or as involved as representing readers' deeper meaning from text. Mapping can be used as a pre-assessment and post-assessment measure to show growth in knowledge, and serves as an excellent review tool for content material. Overall, the flexibility of this strategy is well suited for ELLs.

ENGLISH LANGUAGE LEVEL

Early Production to Proficiency

KEY VOCABULARY
- [ ] category
- [ ] details
- [ ] map
- [ ] title
- [ ] topic

RESEARCH BASE
Barrett, M.T., & Graves, G.F. (1981)

Berkowitz, S. (1986)

Ruddell, R., & Boyle, O. (1984)

Word/Idea Map

When initially teaching this strategy, begin with a simpler form of organization, such as a word/idea map, and then move to more difficult forms. (adapted from Berkowitz, 1986)

Procedure

1. Write the title or topic in a box at the center of the paper. Demonstrate on the board or overhead. (You can make a transparency of the Semantic Map on page 72.) The process should follow that of the Whales example below.

```
┌─────────────────┐
│     Whales      │
└─────────────────┘
```

2. Ask students to skim the reading selection and determine the main topics. Write these main ideas/categories as headings in order around the topic (clockwise). Number and underline each topic/category.

1. <u>Types</u>   2. <u>Size</u>

Whales

5. <u>Swimming</u>   3. <u>Mammals</u>

4. <u>Social Behavior</u>

3. Find two to four important details and write them under the appropriate heading.

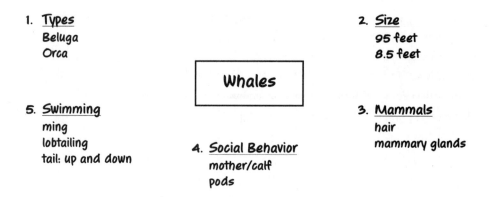

1. <u>Types</u>
Beluga
Orca

2. <u>Size</u>
95 feet
8.5 feet

Whales

5. <u>Swimming</u>
ming
lobtailing
tail: up and down

4. <u>Social Behavior</u>
mother/calf
pods

3. <u>Mammals</u>
hair
mammary glands

4. Draw a box around each category and connect it to the main-topic box.

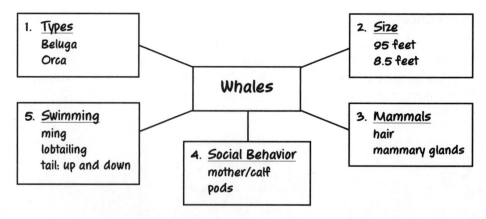

1. <u>Types</u>
Beluga
Orca

2. <u>Size</u>
95 feet
8.5 feet

Whales

5. <u>Swimming</u>
ming
lobtailing
tail: up and down

4. <u>Social Behavior</u>
mother/calf
pods

3. <u>Mammals</u>
hair
mammary glands

5. During and after the lesson or reading, the map can be extended to include new ideas.

6. Students study the map for content, organization of ideas, and review.

Picture Maps

Students can also use pictures to represent words and ideas. This is an excellent format for beginning ELLs. Model this process on the board or overhead using the example below, or one more closely matching your curriculum.

Procedure

1. Decide upon the purpose of the map, such as a list of facts, time line, or cause/effect. Choose a format that best suits the chosen purpose.

2. Choose the important ideas and list them around the title of the picture map.

3. Draw pictures to depict the ideas.

Alternative Procedure for Independent Use:

1. Students write the title (topic) in the center of the map.

2. Student generates a list of words/ideas that are related to the topic.

The Rise and Fall of Cattle Trade in Abilene, Kansas

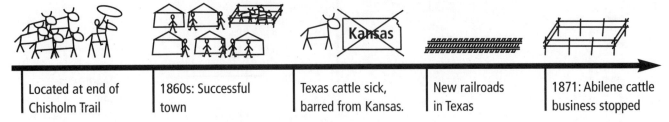

| Located at end of Chisholm Trail | 1860s: Successful town | Texas cattle sick, barred from Kansas. | New railroads in Texas | 1871: Abilene cattle business stopped |

3. Students decide how to organize or classify the list of ideas.

4. Students map these categories around the topic.

5. Students compare and discuss their maps with another person.

6. After their map is complete, students checks to see that all important information is included. If any information is missing, it should be added at this time under the correct heading.

7. Students study their map for a short time. A few days later, they review the map and check for memory. If an item is forgotten, students refer back to the text for verification.

8. Students can use the map as a study tool to review information.

■ ■ ■ ■ ■ ■ ■ Extensions ■ ■ ■ ■ ■ ■ ■

- Use maps as a springboard for writing simple sentences and paragraphs. This is very beneficial for ELLs.

- Use maps as planning sheets to help students organize before writing.

Sample Progress Indicators for MAPPING

Student will:	A	IP	Notes
Link prior knowledge to new knowledge.			
Focus attention selectively.			
Read for comprehension.			
Analyze, evaluate, and show relationships between ideas.			
Represent information visually.			
Interact with others to share information.			
Use the map as a study tool.			

Semantic Map

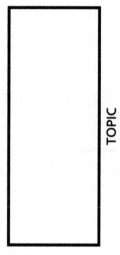

TOPIC

Comprehension Strategies for English Language Learners Scholastic Teaching Resources

Selective Highlighting and Note-Taking

Purpose   The purpose of selective highlighting (in this case, by underlining) is to enable students to differentiate between important information and less significant details. Note-taking provides students with a meaningful structure in which to organize and summarize the content information they hear presented in a lecture or that they read on their own. These two strategies have been combined and presented in sequential order because successful note-taking is dependent upon the student's ability to identify important information (main idea) from supporting details—a skill that is developed through selective highlighting.

Key Benefits for ELLs   When students highlight text, they are actively engaged in a decision-making process. For ELLs who may come to the learning situation with little prior knowledge of a subject, highlighting text helps them determine important versus subordinate information and their relationship to the content. Highlighting also helps ELLs break large amounts of information into manageable units that are easily located within the text. (This activity is particularly helpful when accompanied by a study guide.)

Note-taking is an efficient way for students to organize content information and place it in a meaningful organizational structure. For ELLs who are listening to a lecture, note-taking is a vital skill that they need to acquire. Organizing content information into manageable notes can help students remember important concepts and their supporting details. Notes also serve students well as a review tool and study aid.

ENGLISH LANGUAGE LEVEL

Early Production to Proficiency

KEY VOCABULARY
- boldface
- highlight
- italic
- underline

and any signal words

RESEARCH BASE

Berkowitz, S. J. (1986)

Lapp, D., Flood, J., & Farnan, N. (1996)

Reinhart, S.D., Stahl, S.A., & Erickson, L.G. (1986)

Highlighting

Procedure

Since students are not usually allowed to write in their textbooks, use copied material such as magazine articles, laboratory manuals or reading assignments. To model the strategy (Lapp, Flood, & Farnan, 1996):

> One typical pitfall of highlighting is that students may highlight most of the text. Therefore, it is important to teach effective selective highlighting skills.

1. Copy the content selection (one per student) and make an overhead transparency for your own use.

2. Read the selection aloud and highlight main ideas and important concepts that you want students to learn. Use a "think aloud" technique to demonstrate how you are deciding which information is important. Students should underline their copies as you explain.

3. As you underline, develop basic guidelines with the students for selectively highlighting selections. These can be helpful when students are working independently.

Examples:

- Look for key words and phrases (often in italics).
- Pay particular attention to titles and subheadings.
- Avoid underlining full sentences.
- Carefully study the first and last lines of a paragraph. These often include important information.
- Signal words, such as *because* and *finally* are often followed by important information and indicate their relationship to the content.
- Remember to check graphics or illustrations for key information.
- Try not to highlight more than one third of a paragraph.
- Put an asterisk (*) next to highlighted main points.

■ ■ ■ ■ ■ ■ ■ ■ Extension ■ ■ ■ ■ ■ ■ ■ ■

Have students form groups of two or three. Give each group a transparency that contains a portion of text from their reading assignment. Each group highlights their selection and then presents it to the class for discussion.

Note-Taking

Note-taking can be used by students when listening to a lecture or reading an assignment.

Procedure

1. Instruct students in the use of "language chunks" by demonstrating how to use these single words or phrases to express an idea. This can be done by modeling the process on the board.
   - Choose a sentence and place a check mark (✔) over the meaningful words. Ask students to do the same.
   - Read a short passage or paragraph aloud. Students suggest the main idea in a few words or a phrase and list supporting details in the same manner.
   - Tell a short story and students suggest a title.

2. Teach ELLs how to listen and look for physical cues while you lecture that indicate important information. For instance, students should listen for changes in tone and voice, louder volume, slower pace, and emphatic pronunciation. Body cues include pointing, writing on the board, and emphatic arm movements.

3. Model four types of useful note-taking: simple indentation, two-column format, three column-format, and margin notes.

Simple Indentation (see page 77): This is a simple format that is beneficial when used to introduce note-taking or for students who have problems with organizational skills. This includes writing the main idea using a few words, then indenting and listing the details underneath it.

Example: Simple indentation

> United States of America
>   Democracy
>   Three branches of
>   government
> Executive Branch
>   The president
>   The cabinet members
>   The president's staff
> Legislative Branch
>   The Senate
>   The House of
>   Representatives
> Judicial Branch
>   Supreme Court
>   All federal courts

Two-Column Notes (see page 78): This format provides a simple design for organizing information and fosters self-monitoring of comprehension. Initially, when introducing two-column note taking, it is helpful to use information that the students have selectively highlighted or underlined. Two-column notes are particularly effective for science and social studies and can take a variety of formats including main idea/detail, fact/question, problem/solution, compare/contrast.

- Make a transparency of the selected reading material. Place it on the overhead.
- Give each student a copy of page 78.
- Use a "think-aloud" format and talk students through the note-taking process. You may want to write your notes on the board or another overhead as part of the modeling procedure.

When the process is finished, students can test themselves by covering the information on the right and relating it to the key words on the left. Also, students can use their two-column notes to quiz each other on content information or compare their notes and add any information they decide is needed.

Example: Two-column notes

Topic: Maps

Main Ideas	Details
Kinds of Maps	Topographic: shows land forms Weather: weather bands Physical: geographic features Demographic: population
Map Symbols	Found in legend Compass rose: direction Capitals of countries State capitals Boundaries

Three-Column Notes (page 79): After students have a grasp of two-column note-taking, a third column may be added. Some formats for the third column of notes may be personal response, questions, summary of information, or results. The format depends upon the structure of the lecture or reading assignment.

Example: Three-column notes

What I Know	What I Want to Know	What I Learned

Main Ideas	Supporting Details	Questions

A column for questions is particularly helpful for ELLs. This provides a space for them to note any confusion regarding concepts or language. It is also a "safe" place in which to post questions. In some cultures, it is considered insulting to ask a teacher a question about what was taught.

Margin Notes (in Textbooks and Duplicated Copies): Set aside a few textbooks for ELLs and print margin notes directly on the page that is being read.

- Margin notes should include suggestions for understanding and identifying key concepts and vocabulary and are similar to the ones used in a teacher's guide. For example, in a science textbook notes in the margin next to text might read: "Explains the differences between respiration and photosynthesis." Explain to students that notes in margins are often written in language chunks and not full sentences.

- These notes can also indicate where to find answers. You can draw brackets around the information and note its importance. For example, a note of this type might read: "How many miles is the moon from the sun?"

- When using duplicated copies, encourage students to write their own margin notes and questions that may arise for a certain section of text. This is helpful for ELLs who may have questions regarding vocabulary or meaning while independently reading a selection. This process also helps students keep track of questions or difficulties encountered. You may wish to teach students a simple system of coding text (see page 52).

> Ask parents or volunteer students to copy your margin notes into additional textbooks. This will save the time of having to do duplicate copies.

Traditional Note-Taking

Traditional note-taking in outline form can be very difficult for English language learners if a lecture is not highly organized. If traditional note-taking is taught, first provide a sample outline, exclude some information, and ask students to fill in the missing information. Gradually, exclude more information until students can successfully create their own outline. Remember, ELLs may need to learn additional skills before attempting traditional outlining. These skills include Roman numerals, upper and lower case letters, and cardinal numbers.

Sample Progress Indicators for
SELECTIVE HIGHLIGHTING AND
NOTE-TAKING

Student will:	A	IP	Notes
Use language "chunks."			
Compare and contrast information.			
Represent information visually.			
Synthesize information.			
Take notes from a lecture.			
Make notes from written text.			
Use existing margin notes in text or on copies.			
Write own margin notes on copies.			

Cognitive Strategies

Indentation Notes

Topic: _____

_____

_____

_____

_____

_____

_____

_____

_____

_____

_____

_____

_____

_____

_____

_____

_____

_____

_____

_____

_____

_____

_____

Comprehension Strategies for English Language Learners   Scholastic Teaching Resources

Two-Column Notes

Topic:

Comprehension Strategies for English Language Learners Scholastic Teaching Resources

Three-Column Notes

Comprehension Strategies for English Language Learners Scholastic Teaching Resources

Topic:

Using Graphic Organizers and Signal Words to Teach Text Organization/Structure

ENGLISH LANGUAGE LEVEL

Speech Emergence to Proficiency

KEY VOCABULARY

- graphic organizer
- text structure

Also see individual text structure definitions below.

RESEARCH BASE

Alverman, D. E., & Boothby, P.R. (1986)

Berkowitz, S.J. (1986)

Clark, J.H. (1991)

McCormick, S. (1995)

Purpose   This strategy uses graphic organizers and signal words to teach structural organization of text: Enumeration/List and Describe, Time Order/Sequence, Compare/Contrast, Cause/Effect, Problem/Solution. This helps students to identify the structural organization of a passage and the relationships between text.

Key Benefits for ELLs   Expository text contains complex structures that indicate specific relationships between concepts. Understanding text structure is essential to the comprehension of content. This type of reading and understanding can be challenging for ELLs. In addition to learning new vocabulary, they must decide how all this information fits together. A graphic organizer provides a visual representation of how the text is organized and is an efficient and useful tool when teaching text structure to ELLs. Also, graphic organizers scaffold visualization, a strategy utilized by successful readers. In addition, the inclusion of signal words (see page 83) that indicate the type of structure are very useful when coupled with visual representations. Taking the time to teach text structure along with the corresponding signal words will provide students with tools that support comprehension and apply to numerous content areas.

The following is a description of each type of text structure featured in this lesson:

Enumeration/List and Describe: Lists facts usually by a qualifying characteristic, such as size or importance.

Time Order/Sequence: Uses criteria such as dates and time to order concepts, facts, or events. Can also be cyclical.

Compare/Contrast: Usually compares two general topics comparing similarities and differences between concepts, events, people, facts, and so on.

Cause/Effect: Usually shows change in events, facts, concepts, people, and so on, as a result of something else.

Problem/Solution: Sometimes contains elements of the other organizational structures, such as cause/effect, enumeration, or sequence. The author poses the main elements of a problem and cues readers in to a solution using a cause/effect format.

Procedure

When teaching a specific structure, always teach the coordinating signal words. In presenting the idea of text structure, you can use the analogy of a building structure. This can be quite useful because the analogy is not only familiar to all students but it also lends itself to visual representations (e.g., "How is this text put together? Are some parts built upon other parts? Do the ideas follow in a specific order? What is the relationship of some pieces of information to others?").

1. Divide the class into groups and give each group one article or selection that demonstrates the text structure being discussed. (Newspaper articles are excellent resources for this activity.)

2. Each group is responsible for finding patterns and signal words and explaining relationships between the concepts. Each group should then share its results with the class.

3. Once all the structures are presented, give each group an article or selection that represents a different structure. Groups then share their analyses with the class.

Supplemental Writing Strategy

Procedure

1. Show students several examples of writing (newspaper articles, text, trade books, and so on) that exhibit the structural pattern being taught.

2. Ask students to identify any "signal" words.

3. Then ask them to write a paragraph using the same text structure. Their passage should include appropriate signal words. (You may want to assign specific topics.)

4. Have students share and discuss their writing.

Graphic Organizers

Graphic organizers can be used for all types of text structures (see the collection of graphic organizers on pages 84–91). You can also create your own graphic organizers that are tailored to your students' needs, or use others you may already have on hand. When selecting or creating graphic organizers, use the following guidelines (Merkley & Jefferies, 2000):

1. Analyze the learning task for words and concepts that are important for students to understand. Include signal words.

2. Arrange the words and concepts to illustrate the interrelationships between them.

3. Evaluate the clarity of the relationships as well as the simplicity and effectiveness of the visual.

4. Substitute empty slots for certain words in order to promote students' active reading.

Use the following guidelines when presenting graphic organizers (Merkley & Jefferies, 2001):

1. Verbalize the relationships (or links) among concepts expressed by the visual.

2. Provide opportunity for student input.

3. Connect new information to past learning.

4. Make reference to the upcoming text.

5. Seize opportunities to reinforce decoding and structural analysis, which are critical for ELLs.

Sample Progress Indicators for
GRAPHIC ORGANIZERS AND TEXT STRUCTURE

Student will:	A	IP	Notes
Use graphic organizers to understand relationships between text.			
Identify various text structures.			
Complete the graphic organizer by adding information.			
Recognize signal words and the relationship they represent.			

Signal Words for Text Structures

Enumeration/List and Describe
- first, second, third
- to begin with
- next
- then
- finally
- also
- most important
- until

Time Order/Sequence
- now
- before
- after
- on (date)
- at (time)
- when
- earlier
- always
- later
- into (for example, *into the evening*)

Compare/Contrast
- however
- but
- and yet
- either . . . or
- as well as
- on the other hand
- likewise
- similarly
- not only . . . but also
- although
- yet
- as opposed to
- nevertheless

Cause/Effect
- because
- consequently
- therefore
- as a result
- as opposed to . . .
- if . . . then
- since
- thus
- due to . . .
- led to . . .
- so that

Problem/Solution
- A way this can be solved . . .
- The problem is . . .
- One solution to this . . .
- A solution might be . . .
- An explanation for this . . .
- The challenge is . . .
- The key is . . .
- The answer is . . .
- A resolution for . . .
- The difficulty is . . .
- The trick is to . . .

Cognitive Strategies

List and Describe Matrix

Topic:

Describe:					
List:					

Cognitive Strategies

List and Describe Table

Topic:

Item	Description
1.	
2.	
3.	
4.	
5.	
6.	
7.	
8.	
9.	
10.	

Time Order/Sequence Cycle Graph

Topic: _____

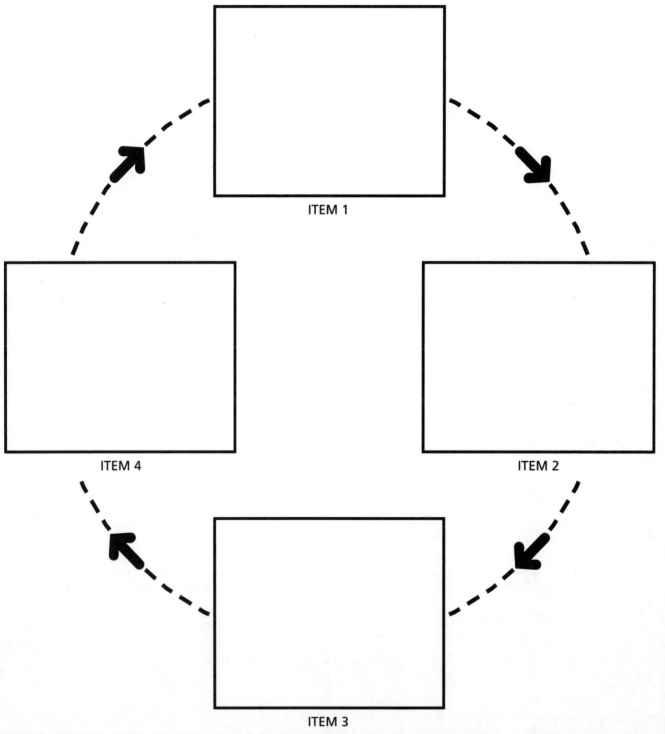

ITEM 1

ITEM 4

ITEM 2

ITEM 3

Cognitive Strategies

Comprehension Strategies for English Language Learners   Scholastic Teaching Resources

Time Order/Sequence Ladder Graph

Topic: _____

Compare/Contrast Diagram

Topic: _____

Item A

Item A and B

Item B

Cognitive Strategies

Comprehension Strategies for English Language Learners   Scholastic Teaching Resources

Compare/Contrast Chart

Topic: _____

SAME			DIFFERENT	
Item 1	Item 2		Item 1	Item 2

Cognitive Strategies

Cause/Effect Diagram

Topic: _____

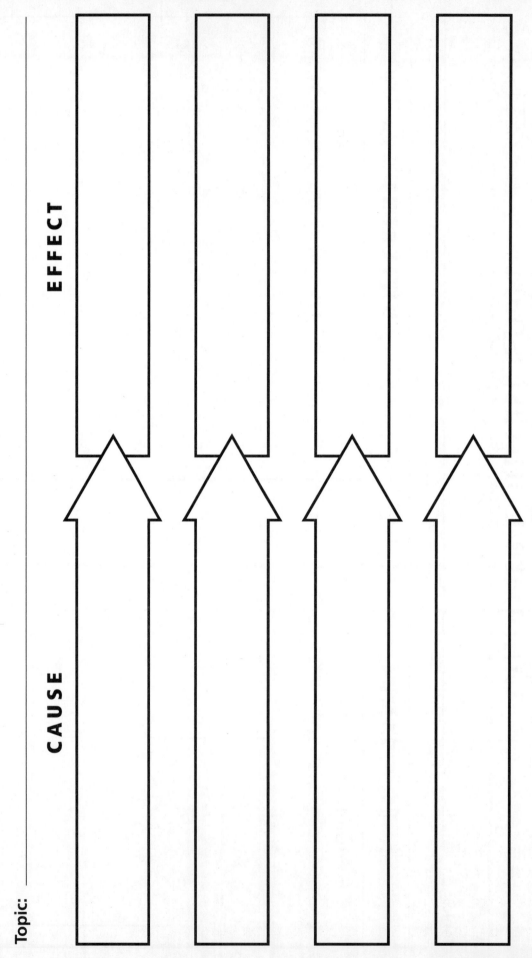

CAUSE

EFFECT

Cause: An act or event that makes something else happen

Effect: A result or product of a cause

Cognitive Strategies

Problem/Solution Diagram

Problem/Challenge

↓

Action Taken

↓

Resolution/Results

Problem/Challenge: Something bad or difficult; a situation that needs to be changed or addressed

Action Taken: What is done to try to solve the problem or meet the challenge

Resolution/Results: What happened as a result of the action taken

Comprehension Strategies for English Language Learners   Scholastic Teaching Resources

Question–Research–Outline–Write!

ENGLISH LANGUAGE LEVEL

Intermediate Fluency to Proficiency

KEY VOCABULARY
- expert
- research
- outline
- question
- statement

RESEARCH BASE

Clark, J. H. (1991)

Glynn, S., Britton, B., & Muth, K. (1985)

Purpose   This strategy gives students an organizational strategy to assist them with content area research and writing. It moves students through the basic steps of forming questions, conducting research, documenting sources, organizing information, and reporting the results in written form.

In this strategy, students develop three questions about a specific topic. They then research the answers and record these on a chart. Then students develop an outline from the questions and information gathered. From the outline, they write an informational passage.

Key Benefits for ELLs   Researching and writing about specific topics is an essential skill for ELLs to master. Knowing how to formulate questions, where to find answers for these questions, documenting, and writing a final report are all skills that students will utilize throughout their academic career. This strategy provides a simple sequential framework for teaching and integrating all of these necessary tasks that are involved in the task of inquiry—perfect for ELLs who are just beginning to learn the skill of nonfiction writing.

Procedure

1. Students generate three questions about a topic. For example, if the topic is Frogs, three possible questions are "What classification is a frog?" "How is a frog different from a toad?" and "What types of frogs can be found in your geographic location?"

2. Students record the questions on the Question-Information Grid (page 93).

3. Then, using three different written sources, students research information related to the questions. Once students become comfortable with this process, they can use two different written sources and one expert interview or response (such as a phone call or letter).

4. Remind students to record the names of the sources and the data found for each question.

5. Students then develop an outline using the information from the grid. While developing the outline, you may demonstrate how to change questions to statements. For example, the question "What classification is a frog?" the statement would become "Frogs are classified as amphibians."

6. Using an outline form as a guide (see page 94), students write an informational passage about the topic.

Sample Progress Indicators for QUESTION–RESEARCH–OUTLINE–WRITE!

Student will:	A	IP	Notes
Follow the sequential steps in the research process.			
Research information from multiple sources.			
Ask and answer questions regarding a specific topic of investigation.			
Request the expertise and knowledge of experts.			
Read and write about subject matter.			
Organize and synthesize subject matter.			

Question-Information Grid

Topic: _____

	Source 1	Source 2	Source 3
Question 1			
Question 2			
Question 3			

Outline

Directions: Fill in the outline. Then use it to help you write an informational passage about the topic.

_____ (Topic)

_____ (Question 1 as a statement)

_____ (Information)

_____ (Information)

_____ (Information)

_____ (Question 2 as a statement)

_____ (Information)

_____ (Information)

_____ (Information)

_____ (Question 3 as a statement)

_____ (Information)

_____ (Information)

_____ (Information)

_____

_____

_____

_____

_____

_____

_____

_____

Comprehension Strategies for English Language Learners Scholastic Teaching Resources

Reciprocal Teaching

Purpose   Reciprocal teaching is a cooperative strategy in which students learn to take on the role of "teacher." Students question, clarify challenges, summarize, and predict to monitor and improve their own comprehension.

Key Benefits for ELLs   Reciprocal Teaching is particularly helpful for ELLs because it is an interactive strategy that promotes comprehension monitoring and question generation, often a difficult task for ELLs. Generating questions supports understanding and identification of question types that can be transferred to the testing situation. In addition, this strategy helps connect pieces of information to the "whole." It also provides an opportunity for students to clarify any difficulties that they encountered while reading the text. It is particularly helpful for ELLs to identify and clarify any language issues that might have arisen. In addition, this strategy gives students an opportunity to practice academic language and behavior, allowing you to assess the level of your own question generation. Be aware that initially for some cultures it may be uncomfortable for a student to play the role of "teacher."

ENGLISH LANGUAGE LEVEL
Intermediate Fluency to Proficiency

KEY VOCABULARY
- identify difficult parts
- predict
- question
- summarize

and any specific content vocabulary

RESEARCH BASE
Palincsar, A.S., & Brown, A.L. (1984)

Procedure

In the initial stages of learning the strategy, it is important for you to model the entire process. After guided practice (when the students understand the process), students can practice this strategy independently in cooperative groups.

1. Select a portion of text. This can consist of duplicated copies or sections of the textbook. In the beginning, it is easier to start with a small section of text—one or two paragraphs.

2. Explain that you will be the teacher first and then various students will take over your part. Then explain the five tasks that will be undertaken:
   1) Read
   2) Question generation
   3) Identify and clarify difficult parts of text
   4) Summarize
   5) Predict what will come next

   Write these steps on the board or overhead. The visuals (page 99) are very helpful for ELLs.

3. **READ**   Both you and students read the assigned passage. If needed, you may read the passage aloud for ELLs.

4. **QUESTION**   Write several questions on the board or overhead. Say, *These are questions a teacher or textbook might ask.* Be sure to begin with a lower level of questioning and work up to more thought-provoking

> The original strategy as developed by Palincsar and Brown (1984) placed the order as Read, Question, Summarize, Clarify/Solve, and Predict. However, for ELLs it is beneficial to identify any difficulties with the reading or questions before they attempt to summarize the passage. Therefore, this slight change in order was made.

questions (Wood et al, 1995). Students answer the questions.

This is an excellent time to teach question types. You may want to focus on the various types of questions on the activity sheet (page 98). These cognitive-domain question types are based upon Bloom's Taxonomy. The order is based on a continuum from lower-level to higher-level thinking skills. Students can put a check mark in the box next to the question types asked. Using this guide, both you and students alike can monitor the level of the questions being created.

- **Recall/Identification Questions:** Student recalls facts or literal knowledge with little prompting or clues.

- **Translation Questions:** Student translates information from one symbolic form or language to another; uses data to fill out a chart, graph, or other graphic organizer.

- **Inference Questions:** Student uses textual information to reach an answer that is not explicitly stated. Includes conjecture—making predictions when all the information is not yet available.

- **Application Questions:** Student uses rules, methods, theories, and facts to answer questions. Also, relates to real-life circumstances.

- **Analysis:** Student answers question by separating the whole into parts and looking for interrelationships.

- **Synthesis Questions:** Students use creative thinking to answer a question.

- **Evaluation Questions:** Requires personal judgment to answer a question.

5. **IDENTIFY DIFFICULT PARTS and PROBLEM-SOLVE**   Model how to identify areas of difficulty. Say, *While I was reading the text, I didn't know the meaning of this word.* Or *This part was difficult for me to understand.* Or, *I'm not sure what this question is asking.* Then ask, *What strategies can I use to solve this problem?* Students offer suggestions. If students have difficulty with this, you may take the opportunity to suggest some strategies.

6. **SUMMARIZE**   Continue the process by saying, *I am going to use the main ideas and supporting details to summarize the reading in this way.* Write the summary on the board or overhead.

7. **PREDICTION**   Scaffold prediction by saying, *Reading and thinking about the selection, I predict the next part will be about . . .*

8. Finally, choose a student to play the role of "teacher" for the next section of text to be read. The student follows the steps above. Offer assistance and feedback as needed. When students seem comfortable, form small cooperative groups that will implement the strategy. By forming smaller groups, more students will be able to serve as "teacher." Give each group member a copy of the Reciprocal Teaching Group Guide (page 99). If students also have a copy of the question types, they can keep a record of the kind of questions being generated during group discussion.

Socio-affective Learning Strategies

Reciprocal Teaching and Writing

After the students are comfortable with the process of Reciprocal Teaching, you can use this strategy to teach writing.

Procedure

1. **Read:** In a small group, students read a short passage of text (or the leader reads it to the group).

2. **Question:** The leader generates questions about the passage. Students then write the questions and their individual answers. They share their responses and make any necessary revisions. Students produce final copies of their answers.

3. **Identify Difficult Parts and Problem-Solve:** Students write down any problems or confusion they encountered while reading or answering the questions. The leader (and group members) help solve challenges. Students write the solutions on their papers.

4. **Summarize:** The leader (teacher) of the group summarizes the text orally. Students then write down the main idea of the summary and supporting details. Each member of the group composes his or her own summary. Students share their individual summaries and make any revisions that are necessary.

5. **Predict:** The leader makes predictions (based upon the reading) about what will happen in the next segment of text. Students then write their predictions and compare them with each other.

> You may want to write Steps 1–5 from the activity sheet on the board or overhead to scaffold students during their cooperative group time. Referring to the illustrations on the activity sheet is also helpful for ELLs.

Sample Progress Indicators for RECIPROCAL TEACHING

Student will:	A	IP	Notes
Participate in whole- or small-group discussions.			
Ask and answer questions.			
Use appropriate language according to audience.			
Formulate questions.			
Make predictions.			
Clarify and support answers.			
Monitor comprehension.			

Question Types

Directions: Put a check mark next to the question types asked.

Question Type	Example
☐ **Identification Questions**	Who? What? When? Where? Which? How many?
☐ **Translation Questions**	Can you describe . . . ? Can you tell in your own words . . . ? What do these symbols represent?
☐ **Inference Questions**	What can you tell from . . . ? What does this indicate . . . ? What do you think will happen? What will the next section be about? What is the main idea?
☐ **Application Questions**	How . . . ? How can this problem be solved? How might a person . . . ? In today's world, how . . . ? Can you explain . . . ?
☐ **Analysis**	Compare/Contrast How are ____and ____ alike? (different?) What are the strengths? Weaknesses? Cause/Effect . . . What caused _____? How does . . . affect . . . ? How does this relate to earlier readings?
☐ **Synthesis Questions**	How would you create . . .? How would you . . . ? Think of a way . . .
☐ **Evaluation Questions**	How do you feel about . . . ? In your opinion . . .

Comprehension Strategies for English Language Learners   Scholastic Teaching Resources

Socio-affective Learning Strategies

Reciprocal Teaching Group Guide

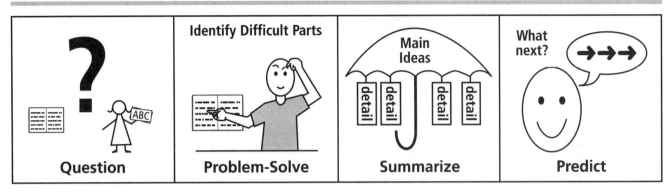

| Question | Problem-Solve | Summarize | Predict |

Group Members: _____

_____

_____

Group Teacher: _____

1. Read: (section, page) _____

2. Questions: _____

_____

_____

3. Identify Difficult Parts: _____

_____

_____

   Solutions: _____

_____

4. Summarize: _____

_____

_____

5. Predictions: _____

_____

_____

Comprehension Strategies for English Language Learners   Scholastic Teaching Resources

ReQuest Procedure

Praise students for formulating questions that resemble teacher-generated questions.

Purpose This procedure provides an opportunity for you to model exemplary prereading questioning behavior and encourages students to set their own purposes for reading. This enables students to become more active, proficient, and independent comprehenders of text.

Key Benefits for ELLs ReQuest is especially helpful for ELLs because it offers them an "expert" model (teacher) and practice in formulating questions that will lead to the comprehension of text. ReQuest also eliminates some of the stress associated with traditional class participation that ELLs may experience. In addition, ReQuest is an effective vehicle for preparing students to become independently successful comprehenders of text. This aids in the understanding of home reading assignments. By using the following procedure (adapted from Manzo, 1969), students will learn how to set a purpose for reading a selection.

Procedure

1. With the same reading selection in front of both you and students, explain that the goal of this lesson is to learn how to set a purpose for reading the selection.
2. Everyone silently reads the title and the first sentence.
3. Encourage students to ask you as many questions as they want about the first sentence, especially those that a teacher might ask.
4. Continue by answering each question but do not elaborate or ask questions back. Be sure books are closed when answering questions.
5. After students have finished questioning, ask them as many questions about the first sentence as is necessary to focus attention on the purpose for which the selection was written and the main question it answers. If students cannot answer a question, encourage them to explain why they cannot do so.
6. Continue the process through the remaining sentences in the paragraph, using the pattern: Silent reading/student questions/teacher questions. Upon reaching the second or third sentence, begin to model questions that integrate elements from previous sentences. For example, you can say, "Thinking about the last two sentences, why did the author use the title 'Caring For Our Nation's Natural Resources'?"
7. After discussing a portion of text, ask students to predict what will happen in the remaining text. Students read and monitor their predictions.
8. ReQuest should continue until students can decode and understand the meaning of all the words in the first paragraph, demonstrate a thorough understanding of the sentences read, and formulate a reasonable purpose

Socio-affective Learning Strategies

for silently reading the rest of the selection.

   For example, to model how to set a purpose for reading a selection, ask: "What question do you think this selection will answer about caring for our nation's natural resources?" Students may respond, "Why should we take care of our natural resources?" Then say, "Let's all read the remainder of the selection and see if we have identified a good purpose for reading."

9. After the reading is completed ask, "Did we identify a good purpose for reading this selection?"

10. When students have become familiar with the strategy, instead of using one sentence, use sections or paragraphs of text for questioning.

Example of ReQuest Strategy

Title and First Sentence
"Caring for Our Nation's Resources"
Since people depend so heavily on natural resources to live their lives, it is important to take care of them.

Student-Generated Question
Q1: What does *depend* mean in this sentence?
Q2: How do natural resources help people live their lives?

Teacher Answer
A1: It means "to rely upon" or "to count on."
A2: Natural resources include the food we eat, materials for houses and clothes, and gasoline for our cars.

You can also add, "That was a good question, one that a teacher might ask."

Teacher-Generated Question
Q1: What is the key vocabulary in this sentence?
Q2: How did you know that?
Q3: What do you suppose the rest of the selection will be about?

You can also add, "Let's read and question each other on the next sentence and see if it helps us decide what the rest of the selection is about."

Student Answer
A1: Natural resources
A2: It is in boldface type. It is also found in the title.
A3: Natural resources? Maybe how to take care of them?

Sample Progress Indicators for
REQUEST PROCEDURE

Student will:	A	IP	Notes
Ask questions.			
Answer questions.			
Read text silently.			
Follow directions.			
Participate in whole-group discussion.			
Develop a purpose for reading.			

Cued Retell—Oral or Written

ENGLISH LANGUAGE LEVEL

Speech Emergence to Proficiency

KEY VOCABULARY

- cued retell
- free retell

and any specific content vocabulary

RESEARCH BASE

Doyle, P.J., et al (2000)

Purpose   Cued retell is a cooperative learning strategy that gives students an opportunity to recall content information that was read, either in an oral or written format.

Key Benefits for ELLs   Cued retell is an excellent strategy for ELLs because it enables them to monitor their comprehension of text while learning to orally communicate the content to another person. This strategy also develops listening skills and provides social interaction. The literacy skills of reading, thinking, listening, speaking, and (if incorporated) writing are included in this learning tool. It is helpful to pair an ELL with a native speaker.

Oral Cued Retell

Procedure

1. Assign a section of text for students to read.

2. Compile a list of key words or phrases from the content information that was read. Write them on the Cued Retell activity sheet (page 104) and make copies for students to use. Be sure that the words are listed in the order in which they appear in the text. It is important to use no more than 20 items.

3. Have students form pairs.

4. Divide the list of words in half. On the activity sheet, List 1 is the top half of the page and List 2 is the bottom half. Each partner has a list.

5. One partner begins to "retell" the content information that was read. The other student who has List 1 checks off the word or phrases as his or her partner says them. Use the "Free Retell" column for this.

6. The first student is done "retelling" when he or she reaches the place that contains the last word of that half. Any words or phrases that were not mentioned are then read to the student by his or her partner. The student then tells as much as he or she knows about the phrases and words that were omitted. Partners can discuss any items that may be unknown by one of the partners and share information. After an item is discussed, it is checked off in the "Cued Retell" column.

7. Students switch roles for List 2. This partner picks up retelling where the other partner left off, using the same procedure.

Written Cued Retell

Students can use the same lists described in the Oral Cued Retell section.

Procedure

1. One student writes down everything he or she can remember about the text that was read.

2. The students exchange papers with or read them to their partner.

3. One partner checks off each item on the cued retell list of key words and phrases that is included in his or her partner's writing, using the "Free Retell" column, and then returns his or her writing paper along with the completed cued retell sheet.

4. Students add any information that was not included. The item is then checked off in the "Cued Retell" column.

5. Students may extend their writing and incorporate other ideas into the writing piece.

Sample Progress Indicators for CUED RETELL

Student will:	A	IP	Notes
Participate in pair discussions.			
Use technical vocabulary.			
Retell information.			
Verbally respond to the retell of a partner.			
Monitor his or her comprehension of text.			

Oral Cued Retell

Say to your partner, "Tell me everything you can remember about the selection we read." Check off each item your partner says in the Free Retell column. Now say, "I will give you these words to help you remember more things. Tell me as much as you can about each one." If needed, share information with your partner. Check it off in the Cued Retell column.

List 1 Words or Phrases	Free Retell	Cued Retell

List 2 Words or Phrases	Free Retell	Cued Retell

Written Cued Retell   Write down everything you can remember about what you just read. Exchange papers with a partner or read your work to a partner. Each partner should check off each item from the list that your partner included. Return the paper to your partner with the list. The items that were excluded should be added to your paper.

Socio-affective Learning Strategies

Comprehension Strategies for English Language Learners   Scholastic Teaching Resources

Peer Tutoring

Purpose   This strategy allows one student who has mastered a skill to teach that skill to another student who has not mastered it.

Key Benefits for ELLs   Research indicates that peer tutoring has benefits for both the tutor and the student being tutored, especially when it involves an ELL. Often the student will ask more questions and take greater risks with a tutor who is closer in age than a teacher. Communication skills are practiced and developed in both participants. Peer tutoring is cost effective and gives you more time to spend on whole-class activities. In addition, peer tutoring develops cultural sensitivity, increases self-esteem, motivation, and promotes adjustment to school.

For students who serve as tutors, research has indicated an increase in their level of skills, motivation, and self-esteem. These student tutors need to be guided to work with English language learners. Many strategies involve the use of peer-assisted learning, and working with an ELL can be very different from working with a native speaker. A little time spent in training and coaching peer tutors will be time well spent for you, tutor, and student.

General Guidelines

- Choose peer tutors who are good students and genuinely interested in performing this task. ELLs need positive role models to emulate. Do not choose a tutor who is a discipline problem, thinking this will improve his or her behavior.

- Some ELLs may be more comfortable working with a tutor of the same sex. In some cultures, this may be a more acceptable practice.

- Peer tutors should receive some reward for their services. Extra credit or community service hours work well.

- Native speakers provide an excellent linguistic model for the nonnative speaker.

- Nonnative speakers who are proficient in English and speak the student's first language are an optimal choice.

- Same-age or cross-age tutors work equally well.

- Provide a place where the participants may work.

- A tutor may work with more than one student.

- Be sure the parents of the tutor are in agreement with their child serving in this capacity.

- The tutor should not be expected to prepare materials for the lesson.

ENGLISH LANGUAGE LEVEL

For Tutor: Intermediate Fluency to Proficiency or Native Speaker

KEY VOCABULARY

- concepts
- tutor

RESEARCH BASE

Fuchs, Fuchs, Mathes, & Simmons (1997)

Johnson, D. (1983)

Mevarech, R. (1985)

- If possible, ask the ELD professional at your school to conduct a training session with the peer tutors focusing upon the methods that are beneficial for ELLs.

- Ask the school counselor to conduct a cultural sensitivity seminar for peer tutors.

- Peer tutoring is most effective for teaching basic skills.

Procedure

Tutoring sessions can be short-term or long-term. Prepare a Peer Tutor Assignment Sheet (page 108) for each tutor before having the tutors follow the procedure below:

1. **Explain objectives.** The tutor should explain the main concept that is to be learned. For example, the tutor can say, "Today, we are going to learn about ____." He or she will find this information on the tutorial worksheet.

2. **Stay on task.** If the student becomes distracted, instruct the tutor to remind him or her of the main topic of the lesson and show what is yet to be accomplished in the lesson (number of problems, questions, pages to read, and so on).

3. **Provide emotional support.** Prompt the tutor to give supportive remarks when an incorrect answer is given, such as "That's not quite right. Let's try again." Or "Good try but I think the answer is different. Let's look." Or "Maybe we can do this . . ." Remind the tutor to avoid put-downs.

4. **Give praise and positive feedback.** Inform the tutor of the importance of giving positive feedback and provide some examples, such as "You're right. Good answer!" or " You're doing a great job learning this!" Ask the tutor to link praise with a specific behavior, such as "Great job! You remembered that equation for . . . " Or "Good! You reduced the fractions to their common denominator."

5. **Encourage verbalization.** Ask the tutor to "think aloud" and encourage his or her partner to do the same. This helps explain the cognitive processes for both. For example, the tutor can say, "If I were doing this I would take . . ." or " I know that George Washington was a General so he probably led the Revolutionary Army." Instruct the tutor to speak at a slightly slower than normal pace. It is also important for the tutor to use formal English and not slang as this is difficult for ELLs to understand.

6. **Allow for wait time.** This is the pause that follows a question, lasting until a student has answered or the teacher speaks. Inform the tutor of the importance of giving his or her partner enough "wait time." This is particularly important for ELLs who must negotiate meaning and language. A good wait time would be approximately three to five seconds.

7. **Be honest.** Instruct the tutor that if he or she does not know the answer to a question to seek help. If help is not immediately available, the tutor should note the question and get an answer as soon as possible.

8. **Continue on.** If the student does not understand a concept after several attempts, the tutor should note the problem and then go on to something else.

9. **Report Progress.** After each session, ask the tutor to complete the Peer Tutoring Progress Checklist (page 109).

Sample Progress Indicators for
PEER TUTORING

Student will:	A	IP	Notes
Use English to interact with a peer tutor.			
Request and share information with tutor.			
Seek assistance from tutor when necessary.			
Ask and answer questions.			
Engage in conversation.			
Determine appropriate language use.			

Peer Tutor Assignment Sheet

Peer Tutor: _____

Student being helped: _____

Subject: _____ Date: _____

Topic: _____

Concepts to be learned:

Vocabulary:

Tasks to complete (activity sheets, chapter questions, math problems, and so on):

Materials to use (textbooks, manipulatives, pictures, and so on):

Special instructions:

Comprehension Strategies for English Language Learners   Scholastic Teaching Resources

Socio-affective Learning Strategies

Peer Tutoring Progress Checklist

Peer Tutor: _____

Student being helped: _____

Subject: _____ Date: _____

☐ We completed the tasks on the Peer Tutor Assignment Sheet.

☐ We did not complete the tasks on the Peer Tutor Assignment Sheet.

Tasks that need to be completed:

_____

_____

_____

☐ My partner understood all the concepts we covered.

☐ My partner did not understand these concepts:

_____

_____

_____

☐ My partner worked well.

☐ My partner did not work well. Please explain:

_____

_____

_____

☐ Can the teacher help you with anything? _____

_____

Other comments: _____

_____

Think–Pair–Share

ENGLISH LANGUAGE LEVEL

Speech Emergence to Proficiency

KEY VOCABULARY

- listen
- think
- pair
- share

RESEARCH BASE

Johnson, D. & Johnson, R. (1984)

Lyman, F.T. (1981)

Rowe, M.B. (1986)

Purpose   The purpose of this simple cooperative strategy is to provide students with a multimode discussion cycle that gives them time to think, share thoughts with a partner, and then share those thoughts with the class.. In this strategy students listen to a question or presentation. You, through a set of cues or signals, indicate the tasks of *thinking* (giving wait time), *pairing* (discussion with a partner), and *sharing* responses (with the entire class).

Key Benefits for ELLs   Educational research has long supported the notion of the positive effects of "wait time" upon the quality of student responses in the classroom. This concept is particularly important for ELLs. Nonnative speakers must first linguistically decipher the question itself and then cognitively form a response to it. This all takes time. Wait time not only offers time for linguistic interpretation of the question but also response formation.Pairing with another student gives ELLs an opportunity to orally share their response with a classmate and receive valuable feedback.

Procedure

1. For this strategy, it is helpful to pair ELLs with native English speakers. Assign pairs before implementing the strategy.

2. Give a cue to *listen* and present a question. This can be in conjunction with a presentation or a reading associated with the lesson. You can introduce Think-Pair-Share any point during a lesson.

See page 112 for suggestions on how to give cues (signals).

3. Next, give the cue for *think*. Students then think about their response to the question. (Give at least 3 minutes of "think" time.)

4. Then, give the signal for *pair*. Students then pair with their partner. The partners discuss their answers and receive feedback from each other. Students may write or diagram their thoughts. (A "Think Pad" made from a small spiral notebook works well for this.)

5. Finally, give the cue for *share*. Students raise their hands and share their response to the question. (You may want to ask them to include their partner's response also.)

Example

After giving a cue for listen, say: "Using the information you already know and from our lesson today, answer this question, 'Why did the dinosaurs disappear from the earth?' We're going to do a Think-Pair-Share activity. Be aware of the signals and when it's time to change tasks."

If this is a first-time experience, take time to explain the strategy and "cues." There are different ways to "cue" responses. You might choose to use hand signals. Or you may use illustrated cue cards (page 112), which helps prompt ELLs.

Variations

Think-Pair-Share can take many forms depending upon the nature of the question and your purpose. Some variations include

Think-Pair-Square: A pair shares their responses with another pair (Kagan, 1990).

Think-Write-Pair-Compare: Students can write their response after the "thinking" period. These are shared with a partner and compared.

Stand-Up-and-Share: The entire class stands and after a student gives a response, he or she sits down and those who agree also sit down.

Sample Progress Indicators for
THINK-PAIR-SHARE

Student will:	A	IP	Notes
Follow oral and written directions.			
Interpret a teacher's command and use appropriate behavior.			
Interact with a partner or in a group.			
Use English to express thoughts and ideas (orally).			
Use English to answer questions.			
Listen to English and employ effective listening skills.			

Think–Pair–Share

Hand Signals

Here are possible hand signals to use for Listen, Think, Pair, and Share.

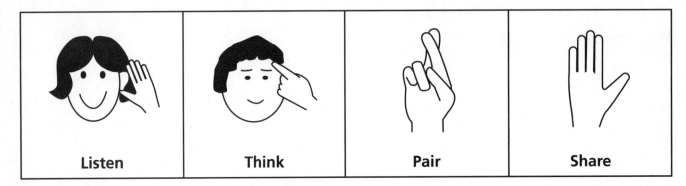

| Listen | Think | Pair | Share |

Cue Cards

Here are possible cue cards to use for Listen, Think, Pair, and Share.
You may want to enlarge these and mount on cardboard.

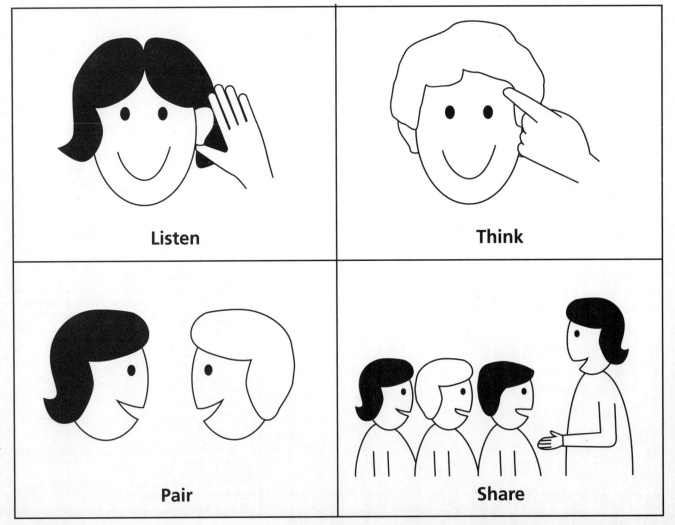

Socio-affective Learning Strategies

Comprehension Strategies for English Language Learners   Scholastic Teaching Resources

Jigsaw Classrooms

Purpose   This cooperative strategy gives students the responsibility for purpose setting, generation of questions, and comprehension monitoring. With this strategy, students become information "experts" and take responsibility for each other's learning.

Key Benefits for ELLs   Originally devised to foster cooperation and increase tolerance and respect among students, this strategy provides an opportunity for students to interact and support one another in a meaningful context. It is particularly helpful to pair beginning level ELLs with a supportive English language speaker. In this way, students can observe, interact, and participate. For more advanced ELLs, this strategy provides an excellent opportunity for orally sharing and paraphrasing text, listening to English academic language, and observing the behavior of mainstream students. This also reduces the reading assignment into manageable chunks.

Since its inception, many forms of jigsaw classrooms have been developed from the original premise. Overall, this strategy gives ELLs an opportunity to participate in group learning, which provides scaffolding and social interaction.

Procedure

1. Place students in groups. Assign a number to each student in the group: 1, 2, 3, and so on.

2. Assign a specific reading passage (or number of pages) to each number. For example, "All number 1's read the first page, all 2's read . . ."

3. Students then read the text that has been assigned to their number.

4. After reading, groups of 1's, 2's, and 3's come together to form an expert group. These expert groups share and discuss their information. They decide how to report it back to their original jigsaw group of mixed numbers.

5. The original groups reconvene and share their information with one another. Each member is an "expert," responsible for reporting his or her part of the information, and answering questions that may be posed by other members of the group.

6. To follow up, the whole class can have a discussion or the individual groups can write a report.

ENGLISH LANGUAGE LEVEL

Early Production to Proficiency

KEY VOCABULARY

- expert
- report
- report back
- responsible

and any specific content vocabulary

RESEARCH BASE

Aronson, D., & Gonzalez, A. (1988)

Aronson, E., Blaney, N., Stephan, C., Sikes, J., & Snapp, M. (1975)

Sample Progress Indicators for JIGSAW CLASSROOMS

Student will:	A	IP	Notes
Explore alternative ways of saying things.			
Follow directions to form a group.			
Negotiate cooperative roles and task assignments.			
Take turns when speaking in a group.			
Negotiate orally to identify role in preparation for a group/class presentation.			
Synthesize and evaluate information.			
Locate information appropriate to an assignment in text.			
Apply basic reading comprehension skills.			
Apply the appropriate style of speech for audience and setting.			
Orally communicate academic information using specific vocabulary.			

Collaborative Reading and Alternative Texts

ENGLISH LANGUAGE LEVEL

Preproduction to Proficiency

RESEARCH BASE

Alvermann, D.E., & Boothby, P.R. (1986)

Gibbons, P. (1993)

Slavin, R. (1983)

Purpose   This strategy allows students of various reading levels to participate in a group research activity and gain information from an array of sources. You may choose books that are best suited to the reading level of individual students.

Key Benefits for ELLs   Enabling ELLs who may not be reading at grade level the opportunity to participate and contribute in a community of learners is invaluable. You can choose appropriate text so that each student feels that he or she is a successful participant in the assigned research task. This strategy provides practice in reading, speaking, and organizing. The opportunity to share information with the group and eventually the whole class, regardless of language or reading ability, builds confidence and helps to establish a sense of belonging in ELLs.

Collaborative Reading

Procedure

1. Assemble a collection of books and articles based upon the content to be explored. Be sure to include books and articles at different reading levels. It is helpful to know the reading level of your students. Consult with the school reading specialist or ELD/ESL teacher to obtain this information.

2. To help you compile a selection of books, see the suggestions for acquiring alternative texts on page 115.

3. Organize students into heterogeneous work groups. Take some time to organize these groups. Consider what characteristics each student will bring to the learning situation. Be sure to include one student in each group who has strong reading and writing skills.

4. Assign a topic or a specific portion of a topic to each group. Then have the groups brainstorm questions they would like answered about their topic and record the questions on a chart or piece of paper. It is helpful for each student to have a copy of the questions. (See the chart on page 117.)

5. Be sure each member of the group has a book on the topic that corresponds with his or her reading levels.

6. Each student researches the answers to the group's questions using his or her individual book or resource.

7. Instruct students on how to find the answers to their questions, take notes, and locate important information.

An excellent resource for determining reading level is *Qualitative Reading Inventory II (QRI-II)* by Leslie, L., & Caldwell, J. (1995). Addison Wesley Longman, Inc. This Informal Reading Inventory assesses the level of expository reading as well as narrative.

8. Construct a data chart. After the members of the group have completed findings and discussed them, ask the group to construct a chart or another graphic organizer and plan how they will present their data to the entire class. Beginning ELLs can share in various ways, such as drawing.

9. Allow time for groups to practice their presentation. This is very crucial for ELLs.

10. Finally, evaluate the group process.

■ ■ ■ ■ ■ ■ ■ ■ ■ ■ Extension ■ ■ ■ ■ ■ ■ ■ ■ ■

Students write a research paper using the data collected from every group.

Alternative Texts

Alternative texts are books and articles (newspaper and magazine) that cover the same subject being studied but are written on various reading levels. The use of alternative texts allows ELLs an opportunity to participate in classroom activities and content learning on a level where they can be successful.

Tips for Using and Acquiring Alternative Texts

■ Engage the help of the reading specialist or ELD/ESL teacher to determine the reading level of the student and the level of text needed to accommodate them.

■ Ask the librarian or media specialist to help you compile a group of books and articles about a specific topic that are written on various levels. These can be kept in your room or in a special place in the library. (Some school librarians have developed a section of "concept or topic" books that are used for this purpose.)

> **Some Sources for Alternative Texts**
> *Adventuring With Books* by Pierce, K., et al (1999)
> Modern Curriculum Press http://www.msschool.com
> Rigby http://www.rigby.com
> Scholastic Publishing http://www.scholastic.com
> Steck-Vaughn telephone: 1-800-531-5015
> Sundance http://www.sundancepub.com
> Wright Group http://www.wrightgroup.com

■ Work with the library staff to obtain quality alternative content books that address the topics to be covered during the school year. Money can be obtained from local, state, or federal grants, a fundraiser; or built into the school budget.

■ Create a "sourcebook" for specific topics. A sourcebook is a collection of writings on a specific topic. Copy articles, illustrations, graphics, and selections from books, the Internet, and magazines and compile them into a collection similar to a course packet. This is particularly helpful for ELLs and can save you many hours of time searching for information. It is beneficial for ELLs if the sourcebooks are developed on varying reading levels.

Using Nonfiction Trade Books

Incorporating nonfiction trade books into your classroom resources can be very beneficial for ELLs. Trade books are written on varying reading levels which allows teachers to provide students with content materials that might be a closer match to the student's appropriate reading level (Hillerich, 1987). In addition, nonfiction trade books are generally rich with illustrations and visual appeal.

Nonfiction trade books also offer an in-depth perspective on a specific content topic. Often, nonfiction trade books are organized more logically than content textbooks and may contain more up-to-date information. In addition, reading additional sources exposes students to varied concepts and expanded vocabulary terms that build knowledge on a topic. These factors are particularly helpful for ELLs.

Tips for Selecting Appropriate Nonfiction Trade Books for ELLs

- Match reading and language level of the student with appropriate text.
- Choose books that are rich in content vocabulary.
- Books should contain quality photographs or illustrations that are realistic.
- Be sure illustrations are well-placed and close to coordinating concepts or vocabulary terms.
- Pages should be well-designed and attractive.
- Information is logically organized.
- The author clearly distinguishes between fact and opinion.
- Book should appeal to students' age level.
- The author should write in a tone that indicates a "real person" is behind the writing.
- It is important for ELLs to have references such as indices, bibliographies, appendices, reference notes, and glossaries.

Some Sources for Nonfiction Trade Books

Ask the school librarian to order specific nonfiction trade books and shelve them in a special section of the library, labeled by topic. Request several copies of the same book, enhancing the opportunity for group work.

Sample Progress Indicators for COLLABORATIVE READING

Student will:	A	IP	Notes
Read and explain data from text.			
Take notes on important information.			
Organize data in a useable way.			
Participate in a group presentation of data.			
Use text organizers to locate information.			

Socio-affective Learning Strategies

Collaborative Reading

Comprehension Strategies for English Language Learners   Scholastic Teaching Resources

Topic: _____

Group Questions:	Group Member: Resource:	Group Member: Resource:	Group Member: Resource:	Group Member: Resource:

Content Rewrites/Adapting Written Text

ENGLISH LANGUAGE LEVEL

Early Production to Intermediate Fluency

KEY VOCABULARY

dependent upon specific text used

RESEARCH BASE

Cooper, J.D., et al. (1999)

Short, D. (1989)

Purpose   This strategy helps you adapt written text so that it is comprehensible to English language learners.

Key Benefits for ELLs   Generally, textbooks are written for native speakers of English. Often, ELLs find these texts and written materials difficult to understand both semantically and syntactically. In addition, some can be culturally biased. By rewriting and adapting written materials, the information contained in them is more accessible to the nonnative speaker. Although this process can be time-consuming, it is well worth the effort.

It is often helpful to form a committee of content teachers who are willing to rewrite text. Each teacher rewrites a section of text. It is subsequently reviewed by fellow committee members and then shared with other teachers. Keep these text adaptations in a file for future use.

Guidelines for Content Rewrite

- New vocabulary should be clearly introduced before reading or defined within the text.
- Use "technical" vocabulary. Vocabulary can be simplified but key terms must be retained.
- Avoid the use of synonyms. These can be confusing to students who are beginning to learn the language.
- Use simple verb tenses, such as present, present continuous, simple past, and simple future.
- Write simple sentences. Avoid clauses. Use the common subject-verb-object format.
- Write in the active voice.
- Use pronouns carefully.
- The topic sentence should be the first sentence in the paragraph. Use the same format for successive paragraphs.
- Keep signal words that indicate the structure of the text. For example, *because* (cause/effect), *likewise* (compare/contrast), *who* (question), *finally* (sequence).
- Ask a colleague to evaluate the text for clarity. (The ELD/ESL teacher is an excellent resource for this.)

Example of Text Adaptation

Discoveries in Ancient Egypt

The kingdom of Ancient Egypt lasted for 3,000 years, beginning around 3100 B.C. Historians often call Aha, also known as Menes (MEE-nez), the first Pharaoh. Many credit him with uniting Lower Egypt and Upper Egypt into one kingdom. Egyptian civilization "took a gigantic leap" under the ruler Aha.

Rewrite for ELLs

Discoveries in Ancient Egypt

The kingdom of Ancient Egypt began close to the year 3100 B.C. Ancient Egypt lasted for 3,000 years. Kings in ancient Egypt were called Pharaohs (FAIR-ohz). Aha was the first Pharaoh. This king was also called Menes (MEE-nez).

Ancient Egypt was divided into two parts called Upper Egypt and Lower Egypt. Aha did an important thing. He united Upper Egypt and Lower Egypt and made them one kingdom. This helped Egyptian civilization move ahead quickly.

Original text adapted from "New Discoveries in Ancient Egypt" by Bryan Brown, *Junior Scholastic*, 107. 18.

■ ■ ■ ■ ■ ■ ■ ■ Extension ■ ■ ■ ■ ■ ■ ■ ■

Make an audio recording of the adapted text and have the student listen to or read along with it. These should be available for both school and home use.

Sample Progress Indicators for CONTENT REWRITES/ ADAPTING TEXT

Student will:	A	IP	Notes
Read and comprehend adapted text.			
Get meaning from context.			
Improve reading skills.			
Master content information using adapted text.			

Leveled-Highlighted Textbooks

ENGLISH LANGUAGE LEVEL

Early Production to Intermediate Fluency

___RESEARCH BASE___

Clay, M. (1979)

Clay, M. (1991)

Smith, F. (1994)

Purpose This strategy enables you to highlight and code a content textbook so that students on varying reading/language levels may interact with written text, questions, and tasks according to their individual abilities.

Key Benefits for ELLs Generally, content textbooks are designed for use with mainstream students who are reading on grade level. Often there is a mismatch between the literacy level of ELLs and the reading level required to successfully interact with the classroom text. You can create a "leveled" textbook by highlighting certain sections of written text and coding questions and tasks. The highlighting is leveled and color coded for each stage of literacy development. The chapter questions and tasks can be coded as well. Students are then assigned reading, questions, and tasks according to their ability. In addition, the answers to questions can be coded in the text, sparing the student from having to search through large amounts of information.

Textbooks

Reserve a few textbooks to use as "leveled textbooks" that can be marked and used for ELLs. You can use a separate book for each reading/language level or books that include all markings for each of the levels. If you choose the latter, tell students to read the appropriate colors. For example, a beginning reader would read only the yellow highlighted text. Form a committee of content teachers who will decide upon the appropriate information to be learned per level. This group will then mark the textbooks. It is helpful to include the ELD/ESL teacher on this committee or seek his or her advice. You may choose to highlight only one or two levels. This is left to the discretion of the committee.

> Once you make a sample highlighted textbook, ask a parent or student volunteers to mark additional copies. (This is a real time-saver.)

Procedure

1. Decide what information should be learned by a student at a specific level.
2. Next, highlight the appropriate text.

   Example

   Level 1, Beginner (yellow): Highlight the title, headings, subheadings, key words and phrases, topic sentence, key words for illustrations/graphics, and topic sentence (if possible).

Level 2, Intermediate (orange): Highlight the title, headings, subheadings, key words and phrases, important captions/graphics, the first and last sentence of each paragraph or summary paragraphs, and significant supporting details.

3. Tell students to read and concentrate upon the information that is highlighted in a specific color. This is the information they will be responsible for learning. For example, "Group 1, read the text highlighted in yellow. Group 2, read the text highlighted in yellow and orange."

4. As students become more successful and proficient in reading, they move to a new level and attempt more of the text. Eventually they will move into unmarked text.

Chapter Questions and Tasks

Form a committee of teachers to assess the questions and tasks at the end of a chapter and assign them to an appropriate level. When choosing questions and tasks, be sure to include some on a higher cognitive plane.

Procedure

1. Place a simple slash mark (/) color coded to the level, next to the questions that the group will answer. For example: yellow (beginner); orange (intermediate) or yellow and orange (beginner and intermediate). Or assign each group a number. Next to each question, write the number of the group that is expected to answer it, for example, 1 (beginner), 2 (intermediate), 1 and 2 (beginner and intermediate)

2. The location of the answers to questions can be marked in the text by placing the question number next to the section of text where the answer is found. Or you can write the page number where the answer is found next to the question. This is very helpful for ELLs in the initial stages of literacy development. Searching an entire chapter for the answer can be time consuming and frustrating for a beginning ELL.

Sample Progress Indicators for
LEVELED TEXTBOOKS

Student will:	A	IP	Notes
Follow appropriate directions for level.			
Read specific material according to level.			
Locate answers and answer questions.			
Gradually move to a higher level.			

Group Reading Inventory (GRI)

ENGLISH LANGUAGE LEVEL

Early Production to Proficiency

RESEARCH BASE

Vacca, R., & Vacca, J. (1989)

Purpose   This strategy allows you the opportunity to assess students' reading based upon classroom texts and the kind of assignments you typically use.

Why Use It?   Because the GRI is flexible and can be administered to a group or an individual student, it provides immediate results based upon the students' interaction with the classroom text. Most textbooks are generally written for mainstream students and the GRI can provide you with information as to how well ELLs can understand and interact successfully with the textbook. It also takes into account the types of assignments and questions characteristic of individual teachers and relates how well the students will handle these tasks. The GRI relates reading assessment to the students' particular learning situation and in this way makes it a very relevant tool for classroom use especially since ELLs generally function at varying linguistic levels.

Procedure

1. Choose a passage that is similar in length, content, and difficulty to the ones that you generally assign to students.

2. Choose the key concepts that students will be required to know after reading the selection.

3. Define the reading skill necessary for the successful comprehension of each concept.

4. Develop a GRI based upon key concepts and reading skills you have identified.

   Example:

Concepts and Skills (for Teacher)
Photosynthesis and Respiration

Key Concepts	Reading Skills
Photosynthesis and respiration are opposite processes.	Compare and contrast the two processes. Focus upon differences. Reading and writing an equation.
Understand and write the equations for both processes.	Translate words to symbols. Know what symbols stand for.
Movement of elements through a plant	Reading a diagram Vocabulary

---

GRI (for Students)

Directions: Read pages 57–63 in your textbook. Then complete the following:

1. **Vocabulary:** Define the meaning of each word as it is used in pages 57–63
   a) respiration
   b) photosynthesis
   c) sugar
   d) chlorophyll

2. **Comprehension:** Write the equations for photosynthesis and respiration. Label each symbol.

3. **Briefly explain** each process. What are the differences between them?

4. **Reading a diagram:** Look at the diagram on page 59. Explain the sequence of the movement of elements through a plant.

---

5. Evaluate students' responses and make conclusions based upon their performance. Do students need more help learning vocabulary? Are the key concepts clear? Can students successfully read a graph? Can they write and translate equations?

■ ■ ■ ■ ■ ■ ■ ■ Extensions ■ ■ ■ ■ ■ ■ ■ ■

■ As the class moves through the textbook, it is helpful to give GRIs throughout the school year.

■ Ask students to write a short summary of the pages they read.

■ GRIs can also serve as study guides.

Sample Progress Indicators for GRI

Student will:	A	IP	Notes
Complete the assigned GRI.			
Follow directions.			
Successfully interact with the textbook.			
Identify skills that will help them read text.			

References

Alvermann, D. E. (1982). Restructuring text facilitates written recall of main ideas. *Journal of Reading*, 25, 754–758.

Alvermann, D. E., & Boothby, P. R. (1986). Children's transfer of graphic organizer instruction. *Reading Psychology: An International Quarterly, 7*, 87–100.

Anders, P. L., & Bos, C. S. (1986). Semantic feature analysis: An interactive strategy for vocabulary development and text comprehension. *Journal of Reading, 29*(7), 610–616.

Armbruster, B. B., & Anderson, T. H. (1981). Research synthesis on study skills. *Educational Leadership*, 37, 154–156.

Aronson, E., & Gonzalez, A. (1988). Desegregation, jigsaw, and the Mexican-American experience. In P. Katz & D. Taylor (Eds.), *Eliminating racism: Profiles in controversy* (pp. 301–314). New York: Plenum.

Aronson, E., Blaney, N., Stephan, C., Sikes, J., & Snapp, M. (1975). *The jigsaw classroom*. Beverly Hills, CA: Sage.

Baker, L., & Brown, A. L. (1984). Metacognitive skills and reading. In P. D. Pearson (Ed.) *Handbook of reading research*. New York: Longman.

Barrett, M. T., & Graves, G. F. (1981). A vocabulary program for junior high school remedial readers. *Journal of Reading*, 24(2), 146–150.

Baumann, J. F., Seifert-Kessell, N., & Jones, L. A. (1992). Effect of think-aloud instruction on elementary students' comprehension monitoring abilities. *Journal of Reading Behavior*, 2, 143–172.

Berkowitz, S. J. (1986). Effects of instruction in text organization on sixth-grade students' memory for expository writing. *Reading Research Quarterly*, 20, 189–202.

Brown, D. (2000). *Principles of language learning and teaching* (4th ed.). White Plains, NY: Addison, Wesley, Longman.

Chamot, A., & O'Malley, J. M. (1994). *The CALLA handbook*. Reading, MA: Addison-Wesley.

Clark, J. H. (1991). Using visual organizers to focus on thinking. *Journal of Reading*, 34.

Clay, M. (1979). *Reading: The patterning of complex behavior*. Auckland, NZ: Heinemann.

Clay, M. (1991). *Becoming literate: The construction of inner control*. Portsmouth, NH: Heinemann.

Cooper, J. D., et al. (1999). *Invitations to literacy*. Boston: Houghton Mifflin.

Cullinan, B. E. (1989). *Literature and the child* (2nd ed.). New York: Harcourt, Brace, Jovanovich.

Cummins, J. (1981) The role of primary language development in promoting educational success for language minority students. In California State Department of Education (Ed.) *School and language minority students. A theoretical framework*. Los Angeles, CA: CA State Department of Education.

Cunningham, J. (1982). Generating interactions between schemata and text. In J. A. Niles & L. A. Harris (Eds.), *New inquiries in reading research and instruction*. Washington, DC: National Reading Conference.

Cunningham, R., & Shablak, S. (1975). Selective reading guide-o-rama: The content teacher's best friend. *Journal of Reading*, 18, 380–382.

Dermody, M., & Speaker, R. B. (1999). Reciprocal strategy training in prediction, clarification, question generating, and summarization to improve reading comprehension. *Reading Improvement, 36 (1)*, 16–23.

Dole, J. A., Valencia, S. W., Greer, E. A., & Wardrop, J. L. (1991). Effects of two types of prereading instruction on the comprehension of narrative and expository text. *Reading Research Quarterly*, 26.

Doyle, P. J., McNeil, M. R., Park, G. H., Goda, A. J., Spencer, K., Lustig, A. et al. (2000). Linguistic validation of four parallel forms of a story retelling procedure. *Aphasiology*, 14.

Dufelmeyer, F. A., Baum, D. D., & Merkley, D. J. (1987). Maximizing reader-text confrontation with an extended anticipation guide. *Journal of Reading*, 31.

Echevarria, J., Vogt, M., & Short, D. (2000). *Making content comprehensible for English language learners*. Needham Heights, MA: Allyn & Bacon.

Enst-Slavit, G., Moore, M., & Maloney, C. (2002). Changing lives: Teaching English and literature to ESL students. *Journal of Adolescent and Adult Literacy, 46*(2). 116–117.

Fielding, L., & Pearson, P. D. (1994). Reading comprehension: What works? *Educational Leadership*, 51(5), 62–68.

Fitzgerald, J. & Noblit, G. (2000). Balance in the making: Learning to read in an ethnically diverse first grade classroom. *Journal of Educational Psychology*, 92(1), 3–20.

Fuchs, D., Fuchs, L., Mathes, P. H., & Simmons, D. C. (1997). Peer-assisted strategies: Making classrooms more responsive to diversity. *American Educational Journal*, 34, 174–206.

Fung, I., Wilkinson, I., & Moore, D. (2003). L-1 assisted reciprocal teaching to improve ESL students' comprehension of English expository text. *Learning & Instruction*, 13(1), 1–31.

Gibbons, P. (1993). *Learning to learn in a second language*. Portsmouth, NH: Heinemann.

Glynn, S., Britton, B., & Muth, K. (1985). Text comprehension strategies based on outlines-immediate and long-term effects. *Journal of Experimental Psychology*, 53.

Graves, D. (1991). *Build a literate classroom*. Portsmouth, NH: Heinemann.

Harvey, S., & Goudvis, A. (2000). *Strategies that work*. Portland, ME: Stenhouse.

Hillerich, R. (1987). Those content areas. *Teaching K–8*, 17, 31–33.

Hudson, F., Ormsbee, C., Myles, B. (1994). Study guides: An instructional tool for equalizing student achievement. *Intervention in School and Clinic*, 30(2).

Irwin, J. (1991). *Teaching reading comprehension processes* (2nd ed.). Needham Heights, MA: Allyn & Bacon.

Johnson, D. (1983). Natural language learning by design: A classroom experiment in social interaction and second language acquisition. *TESOL Quarterly*, 17, 55–68.

Johnson, D., & Johnson, R. (1984). Cooperative small-group learning. *Curriculum Report*, 14(1), 1–6.

Johnson, D., Toms-Bronowski, S., & Pittleman, S. D. (1982). *An investigation of the effectiveness of semantic mapping and semantic feature analysis with intermediate level children*. (Program Report No. 833) Madison, WI: University of Wisconsin Center for Education Research.

Keene, E. O., & Zimmerman, S. (1997). *Mosaic of thought. Teaching reading comprehension in a reader's workshop*. Portsmouth, NH: Heinemann.

Kulhavy, R. W., Dyer, J. W., & Silver, L. (1975). The effects of note-taking and test expectancy on the learning of textual material. *Journal of Educational Research*, 38.

Lapp, D., Flood, J., & Farnan, N. (1996). *Content area reading and learning: Instructional strategies* (2nd ed.). Needham Heights, MA: Allyn & Bacon.

Lyman, F. T. (1981). The responsive classroom discussion: The inclusion of all students. *Mainstreaming Digest*. In A. Anderson (Ed.) College Park: University of Maryland.

Manzo, A. (1969). The ReQuest Procedure. *Journal of Reading*, 12, 123–126.

Martin, D., Lorton, M., Blanc, R., & Evans, C. (1977). *Affective readiness training for teachers and students.* Paper presented at the annual meeting of the Missouri Council of IRA. (Eric Document number ED127578.)

Mayer, R. E, Steinhoff, K., Bower, G., & Mars, R. (1995). A generative theory of textbook design: Using annotated illustrations to foster meaningful learning of science text. *Educational Technology Research and Development*, 43.

McCormick, S. (1995). *Instructing students who have literacy problems*. Englewood Cliffs, NJ: Prentice Hall.

McCracken, R., & McCracken, M. (1995). *Reading, writing, and language* (2nd ed.). Winnipeg, MB: Peguis Publishing.

McKenzie, J. V., Ericson, B., & Hubler, M. (1988). Increasing reading in junior high classrooms. *Journal of Reading*, 38, 452–460.

Merkley, D., & Jefferies, D. (2001). Guidelines for implementing a graphic organizer. *The Reading Teacher*, 54(4), 350–357.

Mevarech, R. (1985). The effect of cooperative mastery learning strategies on mathematical achievement. *Journal of Educational Research*, 78, 372–377.

Meyer, B. J., Brandt, K. M., & Bluth, G. J. (1980). Use of top-level structure in text: Key for reading comprehension of ninth grade students. *Reading Research Quarterly*, 16, 72–103.

Mohan, B. (1986). *Language and content*. Reading, MA: Addison-Wesley.

Muth, K. D., & Alvermann, D. E. (1999). *Teaching and learning in the middle grades*. Needham Heights, MA: Allyn & Bacon.

Ogle, D. (1986). A teaching model that develops active reading of expository text. *The Reading Teacher*, 39, 564–570.

Palincsar, A. S., & Brown, A. L. (1984). Reciprocal teaching of comprehension fostering and comprehension-monitoring activities. *Cognition & Instruction*, 1, 117–175.

Palincsar, A. S., & Brown, A. L. (1986). Interactive teaching to promote independent learning from text. *The Reading Teacher*, 39, 771–77.

Pearson, P. D. (1985). Changing the face of reading comprehension instruction. *Reading Teacher*, 38, 724–738.

Pittleman, S. (1993). Semantic feature analysis: Classroom applications. *Reading Today*, 10(4). 20.

Pressley, M., Almasi, J., Schuder, T., Bergman, J., Hite, S., El-Dinary, P. B. et al. (1992). Transactional instruction of comprehension strategies: The Montgomery County, Maryland, Sail Program. *Reading and Writing Quarterly*, 10, 5–19.

Raphael, T. (1984). Teaching learners about sources of information for answering comprehension questions. *Journal of Reading*, 28, 303–311.

Raphael, T. (1986). Teaching question-answer relationships, revisited. *The Reading Teacher*, February, 516–522.

Readence, J. E., Bean, T. W., & Baldwin, R. S. (1988). Pre-reading strategies-anticipation guides. In *Content area literacy: An integrated approach* (6th ed.). Dubuque, IA: Kendall/Hunt.

Reinhart, S. D., Stahl, S. A., & Erickson, L. G. (1986). Some effects of summarization training on reading and studying. *Reading Research Quarterly*, 21, 442–438.

Rosenshine, B., Meister, C., & Chapman, S. (1996). Teaching students to generate questions: A review of the intervention studies. *Review of Educational Research*, 66, 181–221.

Rowe, M. B. (1986). Wait time: Slowing down may be a way of speeding up! *The Journal of Teacher Education*, 31, 43–50.

Ruddell, R., & Boyle, O. (1984). A study of cognitive mapping on reading comprehension as a means to improve summarization and comprehension of expository text. *Reading Research and Instruction*, 29, 12–23.

Santa, C., Dudley, S. C., & Nelson, M. (1985). Free response and opinion-proof: A reading and writing strategy for middle grade and secondary teachers. *Journal of Reading*, 28, (4) 346–352.

Short, D. (1989) Adapting materials for content-based language instruction. ERIC CLL Bulletin (13) 4–8.

Skehan, P. (1991) *A cognitive approach to language learning*. Oxford: Oxford University Press.

Slavin, R. (1983). When does cooperative learning increase student achievement? *Psychological Bulletin*, 94.

Slavin, R. E. (1997). *Educational psychology: Theory and practice* (5th ed.). New York: Allyn & Bacon.

Smith, F. (1994). *Understanding reading*. Hillsdale, NJ: Erlbaum.

Snap, J., & Glover, J. (1990). Advanced organizers and study questions. *Journal of Educational Research*, 83(5), 266–271.

Tierney, R. J., Readence, J. E., & Dishner, E. K. (1985). *Reading strategies and practices: A compendium* (2nd ed.). Boston: Allyn & Bacon.

Vacca, R., & Vacca, J. (1989). *Content area reading*. Glenview, IL: Scott Foresman.

Vygotsky, L. (1962). *Thought and language*. Cambridge, MA: MIT Press.

Wood, K. D. (1989). Using guided imagery to enhance learning. *Middle School Journal*, 21(2).

Wood, E., Woloshyn, V., & Willoughby, T. (Eds.) (1995). *Cognitive strategy instruction for middle schools*. Cambridge, MA: Brookline.

Sample Progress Indicators

Sample Progress Indicators for

Student will:	A	IP	Notes

Sample Progress Indicators for

Student will:	A	IP	Notes

Comprehension Strategies for English Language Learners   Scholastic Teaching Resources